The Victor Transformation

Elizabeth Louis Creecy
Renew Ministries

TRILOGY CHRISTIAN PUBLISHERS
TUSTIN, CA

Trilogy Christian Publishers
A Wholly Owned Subsidary of Trinity Broadcasting Network
2442 Michelle Drive
Tustin, CA 92780

Rights Department, 2442 Michelle Drive, Tustin, CA 92780.

Trilogy Christian Publishing/TBN and colophon are trademarks of Trinity Broadcasting Network.

Cover design by: Jeff Summers

For information about special discounts for bulk purchases, please contact Trilogy Christian Publishing.

Manufactured in the United States of America

10 9 8 7 6 5 4 3 2 1

Library of Congress Cataloging-in-Publication Data is available.

ISBN: 978-1-63769-906-5

E-ISBN: 978-1-63769-907-2

Contents

Dedication

I dedicate this book to every lost, hurting, and tired soul out there who still believes they can be free from their emotional, physical, and spiritual pain. To every individual who is hungry, desperate, persistently seeking answers, and diligently looking for truth and freedom from their thoughts, beliefs, past pains, and self-hatred. Please do not give up! The answers are found in Jesus Christ!

Preface

Hey! My name is Elizabeth Louis Creecy, and I wrote this book to empower and tactically show people how to live victoriously and walk out of the victim mindset. I wanted to provide people with clear, applicable steps to transform their thinking from victim to victor!

I spent my twenties searching and looking for answers in *all* the wrong places. At the time, I was suffering from a victim mindset. I hated what that mindset was doing to my life. My quality of life sucked! It stole so much life from me. I struggled with constant fear, worry, and anxiety to the point where I would hide in my apartment or drink my feelings away. I had zero self-confidence, and I felt like my only purpose in life was to have sex or be pretty. I know, pathetic, right?

I was hurting. I was confused about my past, and I was desperate for freedom. But I had no idea how to get it. Let alone come to terms with the dysfunctional, toxic, and at times abusive childhood I endured. I went to therapist after therapist searching for the application of getting free, but never found it. Instead, it seemed like they wanted to keep exploring my past, where I was after the techniques that I could implement, allowing me to transform myself. Therapists, after therapists, would confirm that my childhood was abusive but would never provide me with the application of getting free. It sometimes felt like therapy made me feel worse, not better about myself. I wanted to heal, not to constantly reopen my wounds. Finally, I became sick and tired of the charades. I decided to earn a master's degree in positive psychology, thinking maybe all the therapists I went to didn't understand what I was trying to understand.

I was relentlessly after freedom! I was not going to stop looking for it until I found it. I was hungry for freedom! I mean real freedom, where coping was not part of the equation. I wanted freedom from my past pains. I wanted to experience everlasting joy, peace, and victory. I wanted to feel like a winner, not a loser. I wanted to feel unconditional love, important, worthy, and secure regardless of what was happening externally around me. I wanted to restore my family relationships forever, forgiving my mom and brother for some of their cruel actions. Guess what? I found it. I found freedom, but it was not where I thought it would be.

When I started doing life the Jesus' way, my entire world changed. Jesus took all my pains from me to the point where I have to think consciously about my past to remember them. Let me tell you—it feels awesome! Whereas when I was in bondage to the victim mindset, those painful memories would haunt me every second, keeping me in bondage too paralyzed to move, buying the lies that I would never escape the mental torture. But praise Jesus because nothing and no one is more powerful than Him. He broke my chains and gave me freedom and victory! I finally found what I was after, and it was better than I imagined!

My entire life, I have been an advocate for people. As a kid, I would stand up to bullies. Perhaps it was because I couldn't stand up to the bully in my house. Nonetheless, I have always wanted to save people. I hate seeing suffering. So, when I noticed how many people were walking around with the same pains, fears, and struggles I had while under the oppressing victim mindset, I decided to do something about it. I began retracing every step I took with Jesus that led me to change my victim mentality to that of a victor, which is how I created *The Victor Transformation!* This book encompasses everything I first began doing to tear up my mental garden of weeds and dead fruit, to preparing the land to plant seeds of life. You will notice there is some psychology, neuroscience, and neurotheology in here too. However, I only believe in the psychology, neuroscience, and neurotheology that honors what Jesus says!

When I tell people about the crap I have overcome, most people are amazed. Abuse is an ugly word that can mean so much and so little all at once. Abuse is never okay but is very common. Perhaps you, too, had an abusive past. Like many, my childhood had many ups and downs filled with psychological, emotional, and occasionally physical and sexual abuse. I have been drowned, strangled, shot at, knife to my throat, neglected, molested by many men, raped, and almost died from a life-threatening eating disorder, to name a few. It all started after I suddenly lost my dad at age seven. After my dad's death, it seemed like the rest of my family died over the next ten years. Quickly death became normal to me as I went to funeral after funeral either weekly, monthly, or every few months. One day my uncle and grandfather died within hours apart. Death, darkness, evil, tragedy, pain, and hardship infused my childhood, and it felt like I could never escape it.

I no longer have any bitterness towards those who have hurt me. I truly forgive my perpetrators, especially my mom and brother. Today my relationship with my mom is completely restored, and my brother and I are in a much better place. One of the biggest challenges for me when writing this book was navigating the delicate dance of being honest about what I endured as a child, wanting to protect my mom and brother from judgment, not writing it in a woe is me tone. While clearly articulating the pure forgiveness and love I have for them. I love them very much, and I ask you not to judge them but separate their sin from their being. Besides, don't we all fall short? Haven't we all sinned? If anything, maybe this book will encourage you to forgive all who have hurt you!

For years I was very angry and bitter, but I now see I was only hurting myself and buying the lies from the devil. Paul tells us in Ephesians 6 that we do not fight against flesh and blood but against evil spirits. It is so true. The people who hurt me were dealing with their own evil within them that unfortunately impacted me greatly. Since I got hurt, I hurt people too. By no means was I perfect and free from sin. When Jesus showed me, I do not need to be angry at them but the spirits within them, things became much easier to navigate for me. In Philippians, Paul writes about how his misfortunes became his fortune. I can attest to that. I was so angry about my past until the Lord started showing me that my misfortunes are some of my greatest fortunes. My past taught me a lot about life, gave me tremendous life experience, and resulted in some of my greatest strengths like resilience, empathy, forgiveness, and understanding people at a profound level. However, the fortunes from my childhood pains led me to discover God's purpose for my life. I believe I am to empower people to be Warriors for Christ by helping them renew their minds to the Word of God and teaching people how to navigate mental health and emotional wellbeing from a biblical perspective. God can use every part of your life if you let Him. Again, I am living proof of this.

Additionally, this book is not about the pains of my past but the redemptive power of Jesus Christ. It's my prayer that when you read this book, you do not see anything but the power of the Holy Spirit. I pray you walk out of bondage and learn the valuable things you can implement in your life to advance God's will in your life.

I have intentionally written this book to allow you to turn to any topic, read it and understand it with ease. I hope you see this book not as self-help but as a Jesus-help. Allow this book to be a guide that teaches you how to carefully renovate your mental garden, empowering you to intentionally start planting mental seeds of life, nurturing them, and in time seeing a prosperous garden bloom. You do not have to stay chained to any path or way of thinking. Life is a bit like the game Shoots-and-Ladders. At any point, you can turn around or jump to another path. Please don't believe the lies that scream you cannot change your ways or life because you can—I am living proof of this. If I can change my life with the help of Jesus, you can too.

Here is a more excellent way!

"Wait patiently for the LORD. Be brave and courageous.
Yes, wait patiently for the LORD"
(Psalm 27:14, NLT).

The Victor Transformation: Introduction

Hello, and welcome to *The Victor Transformation!* In this book, we will create the space and security to transform your victim mindset or toxic thinking into a mindset of a *victor*. I will provide you with understanding, tools, techniques, and exercises to help you pull up the weeds of the victim mindset, plant godly seeds of hope, joy, peace, and positive thinking so you can develop a victorious way of thinking. While those seeds are essential, the most crucial part of this journey will be creating a solid relationship with the Godhead: the Father, the Son, and the Holy Spirit. It is in that relationship that your life will begin to transform, and you will see that the victory has always been yours. I hope that this book blesses you to successfully throw out the victim mentality and step into living as a *victor* through Jesus Christ!

It is through Christ that you are a victor and have everlasting freedom! Apostle Paul tells us in 1 Corinthians 15:57 that the Father gives us the victory through our Lord Jesus Christ. If you have confessed with your mouth that Jesus is Lord and believe in your heart that God raised Jesus from the dead, you will be saved (Romans 10:9). Through that confession, you become a new person and enter the body of Christ, where you always have victory! Are you ready to learn how to be that new creation in Christ and rid yourself of the bondage your enemy is hoping to keep you in?

Throughout the Word of God, there is a spoken and unspoken theme that declares all those who follow the Lord to be *victorious*! Perhaps right now, you feel alone, abandoned, hopeless, depressed, angry, exhausted, overwhelmed, and petrified of your past, present, and future. Essentially everything but victorious! Maybe you feel like you cannot get a break and yearn for the days where God's everlasting joy, peace, hope, and optimism fill your heart. If you are willing and open to doing things God's ways, your life can quickly transform. Now, you will have to do your part, but it is easier than you think.

If you don't believe that you are a *victor* in Christ, then I pray the Holy Spirit brings this verse to life for you: "For the LORD your God is going with you! He will fight for you against your enemies, and he will give you victory!" (Deuteronomy 20:4, NLT) It is easy to feel outnumbered and like there is no way out or no possible victory insight. I get it. The Israelites even got it. You are not helpless, but we must get you thinking differently and seeing yourself as God sees you. Just as the Father encouraged and strengthened the Israelites' confidence by reminding them that He was always there for them and would save them from any potential dangers they faced. The Father wants to do the same for you! Remember, nothing is stronger than the power of the Holy Spirit, so when you consider that all things are possible with the Father (Luke 1:37) and that He can overcome every possible odd, you too can feel secure by placing your trust and faith in Him. The question is, are you going to let the Father in and obey His ways? Let's be real; your way is not working! What do you have to lose by trying it the Father's way?

You see, not everyone knows how to live and think like a victor! You might be even wondering what a victor is? A *victor* loves the Father, delights in the Word of God, believes in God's promises, is led by their Spirit Man, and operates from the mind of Christ. I hope this book provides insight and resources to help your spiritual eyes of understanding become enlightened to the marvelous and supernatural power that comes when you follow Jesus Christ.

Why Do People Adopt the Victim Mentality?

People fall into a victim mindset because of what seems like a rabbit hole that leads to chronic insecurity. In this book, I will also explain the spiritual components that help enforce this belief system: feeling unloved, helpless, insecure, and like everyone is out to get you. Ultimately know the devil's schemes are tricking you. The victim mindset is a vicious cycle that causes the individual to push people away unintentionally and unconsciously, live in a disempowering state of mind, and have an inferior quality of life. But why—why do some people do this?

It is typically due to multiple components like evil spirits, soul wounds, trauma, fear, and a belief that you are not good enough, loved, or worthy. All this comes from the devil. Unfortunately, it can be easy to buy his lies but know they are just lies. I hope that this book helps you identify and untangle the lies he has sold you so that you can then destroy them through your authority in Christ.

Understand that Jesus even warns us that as long as we are on earth, we will face persecution, suffering, and life pressure. However, He concludes that verse by saying, *"It's okay, though. You can be encouraged by Me because I have conquered the fallen world. Just keep your eyes on Me, and you will have victory."* The question then becomes: are you going to focus on the pain you have endured or the joy and power of Christ Jesus?

"I have told you all this so that you may have peace in me. Here on earth you will have many trials and sorrows. But take heart, because I have overcome the world."
John 16:33 (NLT)

The devil will use anything and everything to destroy us! He hopes that if he can keep us oppressed, the Lord can't use us because we will choose to stay locked in our mental prison cell, desperately hoping someone would rescue us! If the devil can, figuratively speaking, keep you in prison or the ICU of the hospital, you are not a threat to him.

Here's the thing, you hold the key and the power to not believe or listen to that lying scoundrel. Your enemy will tell you, you are powerless, but that is a bunch of baloney. One of the ways the devil likes to get us is when we are very young, and I believe one way he does this is through what is known as soul wounds, which I will discuss in a later chapter.

We have all been hurt. We have been made fun of or called names. Some of us may have been put down, either to our face, behind our backs, or both. However, it's the most painful, the most damaging, and the most hurtful when the offenders are the ones society says are supposed to protect us. When our parents, siblings, spouses, grandparents, or caregivers hurt us, it is far more damaging to us than when a friend, colleague, or peer hurts or abuses us. With a loved one, you have invested more of yourself. You have allowed yourself to become vulnerable. You have greater trust in that person because there is a deep intimacy in that relationship, and when that trust is broken, it can be soul-crushing.

Perhaps you have noticed the unspoken expectations placed on these deep, personal relationships that say a loved one is supposed to want what's best for you and never hurt you. You wouldn't be wrong. Therefore, when a person you regard as a vital source of love, comfort, protection, and care rejects you, hurts you, or betrays your trust, the wound is deep, and when there is more to lose, there will be more pain.

The Victor Transformation will bring awareness to how you may have developed a victim mindset and, most importantly, how to overcome the *"woe is me"* phenomenon into living victoriously through Jesus Christ.

I hope and pray this book empowers you to move from living in your past to living in the present with your eyes locked on Jesus. You will accomplish this by overcoming shame, fear, fixed mindsets, limiting beliefs, and learning the power of love, getting to know yourself, the authority Jesus has already given you, and successfully wearing God's armor. By the end of this book, you will be planning for a prosperous future. You will understand how you can operate in the mind of Christ, and you will know that your fight is not with other humans but with the evil spirits and principalities of the unseen world that manifest in human beings.

I want to be quite clear about one thing! You do not need to come from a traumatic background to reap the benefits of this book. Many people struggle with a victim mindset who have never faced trauma. Ironically, much of the world encourages and pushes a victim's thinking, so it's standard for most people to have some level of this thought process related to a victim mentality.

Are you ready to stop doing things the world's ways and to try something new?

And do not be conformed to this world [any longer with its superficial values and customs], but be transformed and progressively changed [as you mature spiritually] by the renewing of your mind [focusing on godly values and ethical attitudes], so that you may prove [for yourselves] what the will of God is, that which is good and acceptable and perfect [in His plan and purpose for you].
Romans 12:2 (AMP)

The Book Benefits Are

You will learn and benefit from the following topics:

1. How a victor thinks.
2. You will acquire the skills to channel pains and life tragedies into motivation to propel you forward by surrendering them to Christ.
3. Discover how to let go of the past.
4. Start to develop a healthy belief system.
5. You will expand your mental resilience to handle life setbacks.
6. Learn robust and healthy coping mechanisms.
7. How to live in the present and plan for a prosperous future and how to achieve it.
8. Begin to walk as your authentic self.
9. Identify your potential and where you lack in life.
10. Increase your faith, hope, and spirituality.

It's going to be incredible, and all I ask from you is to take one page at a time. While there are some exercises that you can do throughout, please do not feel like you must do them. Think of the exercises as a bonus. Additionally, please do not feel like you have to read this book straightforward. It might make more sense if you do, but I have tried to lay this book out to guide you as you navigate the transformation, meaning at any point, you can read a section without reading what came before it and still have a strong understanding about what is written.

There may be times where you want to quit but push through it! Paul tells us in Philippians 4:13 that you can do all things through Christ Jesus who strengthens you!

"For I can do everything through Christ,
who gives me strength"
(Philippians 4:13, NLT).

That means that you can do everything in God's will for your life. God wants you free from bondage. He wants to fight your battles and do most of the work for you too. When you surrender your life to Christ and strive to live the way Christ asks you to live in God's Word, the Godhead will do most of the work for you! All He needs is an open and willing heart. Please trust me—the Father wants you to operate in the mind of Christ, display the attitude and behaviors of Christ, and be free from oppression, pain, and sickness. Please know you can do this because you are created in God's image (Genesis 1:27). In times where you want to quit or give up, recite Philippians 4:13. You can do this because God wants you well. He wants you to trust Him and to do His will for your life!

Before we dive in, I encourage you to get the following materials to help you succeed:

You will need a journal. I have a few journal exercises for you to do. Plus, I want you to get used to journaling. Journaling is a powerful tool to decompress, cope with a situation, and reflect on your past choices. I believe the ability for the human mind to reflect is one of the greatest attributes the Father gave us, as Paul reminds us in 1 Corinthians 11:28.

Additionally, you will need a Bible. I will provide you the verses, but you must do some work here too. I encourage you to highlight verses and start reading your Bible in general. We have a relationship with Jesus through the Word of God.

"That is why you should examine yourself before eating the bread and drinking the cup"
(1 Corinthians 11:28, NLT).

Exercises

1. Seeing Myself as a Victor:
    a. Begin creating the mental picture or vision of you free from a victim mentality. Find time each day to imagine yourself living as a victor!
    b. Imagine yourself living victoriously through Christ. What comes to mind? Describe yourself as a victor. What words do you speak? What thoughts do you have?

   c. What do you need to let go of or learn to help you see yourself as a victor?

   d. Can you see yourself free from a victim mentality? What would you do? What do you need to stop and start doing to allow yourself to see yourself as victorious through Christ Jesus?

2. Deciding My Path: once you see yourself as a victor, let's get intentional.

   a. Identify three areas in your life from the list below where you struggle the most with the victim mindset. For instance, is it when life doesn't go your way? Or when you hear constructive criticism?

   b. Next, identify a path to begin consciously responding with a victor mentality. Remember, the Father calls us to be a doer of the Word of God. Having a plan to proactively change your thinking and renew your mind to God's Word is a big part of this. You cannot be passive if you want to get free from the victim mentality.

   c. Identify a verse in the Word of God that you can recite when you need to respond differently than you have.

Example: Suppose I identify with a poverty mindset (Fear of poverty), and I want to develop a prosperous mindset. Every time my mind reminds me I don't have enough, I will recite Philippians 4:19 (NKJV), which says: "And my God shall supply all my needs according to His riches in glory by Christ Jesus."

Column A: Victim's Response	Column B: Victor's Response
Is secretly hoping for someone to rescue or save them from their life.	Thinks like a warrior. He/she has the confidence, mental strength, and emotional maturity to change their life or ask for help.
Focuses on the past and struggles to believe they'll have a healthy future, *lost*.	Focuses on the present and plans (*believing*) in their prosperous future.
Lack of mental resilience (*emotions control them*).	Strong foundation of mental resilience and overcomes setbacks (*acknowledge emotions but controlled by values*).
Setbacks defeat them.	Setbacks are viewed as an opportunity for their growth.
Scarcity, poverty mindset (*pessimistic*).	Prosperous, abundance mindset (*optimistic*).

Destructive behavior when in need of coping.	Healthy coping mechanisms.
Holds on to their emotional baggage.	Free from past baggage.
Believes they can't do anything, lost.	Knows their potential and applies it.
Doesn't know who they are. Allows their traumas to define them.	Lives as their authentic self.
Relies on self-will to conquer everything.	Relies on faith, hope, and spiritual component in their life.

Encouragement: You were born with a specific God-given purpose. There is something only you can do and offer this world. Remember, there is no one else like you. Even identical twins have different fingerprints. You must choose to break the agreement you made with the victim mentality (the devil) and come into agreement with the thoughts of a victor! Focus on growth, no matter how small or big. Keep encouraging yourself and know that all things are possible with God, and He is with you!

Prayer: Father God, I come to you in need of your help, love, and forgiveness. I may have been participating with a victim mentality, and I don't want it anymore. If I act like a victim, please show me those times, and help me let go of those tendencies, beliefs, and thinking patterns. Please enlighten my spiritual eyes to help me see the lies I have been buying from the devil. Forgive me for agreeing with the devil and change my heart to see myself as You see me. Father, I am ready to live in the promises You have given me, but I have no idea how to do that. I come to You asking for Your help to teach me, show me, and guard me as I learn how to do life Your way and Your will for my life. I ask that you highlight everything in me that is not of You and take it from me. Please help me to be more like Christ in every way. I open my heart to You. In Jesus' name, amen.

CHAPTER 1

Understanding the Victim Mindset

Ah, I must say I am excited to dive into this chapter with you. Before we begin, please note the first three chapters may come across as choppy. This is so I can outline the foundational information in the most simplistic way allowing for you to build on them.

I will unpack what a victim mindset is and then compare victim thinking to the thoughts a victor would have in the same situation as one who thinks like a victim. I will also help you understand how this victim mindset, or toxic thinking, potentially, even came about in you. You will learn what a victor mindset is and how to apply it in your life. Additionally, at the end of this chapter, you will see a few exercises that will help you grow your awareness and encourage you to start to let go some of your emotional baggage.

For me, when I was finally ready to let go of the emotional baggage I had been carrying for years, I envisioned myself leaving those bags at a bus station and walking away from them. I no longer needed them with me. I realized surrendering my baggage to Christ outweighed the value and comfort of keeping them to myself.

For some reason, I kept believing holding on to those bags was protecting me somehow. I needed a mental metaphor that I could connect with at the time because while I wanted to live for Jesus, He was not yet real for me to the degree He is now. However, the image of driving down to the bus station and leaving them was an image and metaphor I could connect with, see, and understand. Perhaps that imagery will help you let go of your baggage, and you can do the same when you are ready.

"The LORD is close to the brokenhearted;
he rescues those whose spirits are crushed"
(Psalm 34:18, NLT).

The Victim Mindset

As I was researching this book, I learned how simple it is to develop a victim mentality. One does not even need to have ever gone through a traumatic event to establish such a way of thinking. It's my personal belief that when we are children, especially little girls, we are taught to have this thinking that screams, *"Get destressed and wait for prince charming to rescue you."* Such garbage! What I learned from my abusive childhood, walking out of Complex Post Traumatic Stress Disorder (C-PTSD), and living victoriously is that one needs to learn how to believe, depend on, and trust entirely in Lord Jesus. Yes, people will fail you, but the Father never will. You might not understand why He does what He does, as His ways are very different from yours or the world, but He will only ever give you life.

Until I became proactive and changed my thinking, I kept waiting, wishing, and hoping for someone to rescue me, that I even found myself in some foolish situations. Here's the thing, my self-focused, self-absorbed, prideful thinking was destroying me. Believe it or not, the emphasis of "self" comes from the devil, who wants you to be and remain self-righteous (*pride*). Think of it this way, Jesus first focused on what His Father wanted Him to do, then how He could serve others, and then Himself. Therefore, if the enemy can keep you thinking about yourself and that the world revolves around you, then he has successfully kept you from living righteously and agreeing with the Father's will for your life.

Additionally, if you believe you don't need anyone and that no one cares, you will remain the devil's lunch. You see, God wants you to live, think, and be righteous, which means right standing with Him. To be in good standing with the Father, you have to do things His way.

He wants you to do things His way because His way is the only way that gives you life and freedom. It is a freedom that no one can take from you either. That's cool when you think about all the things in your life you worry about protecting and keeping, like money or material goods.

Perhaps you are reading this book because you did experience a miserable childhood filled with abuse. Or maybe you were never taught how to exhibit emotional intelligence or kingdom principles. Whatever caused you to adopt such thinking, know, by the end of this, your thinking will change if you so allow it too. You must do the work; no one can do it for you. God will not bless sin!

What Is a Victim Mindset?

The victim mindset is composed of beliefs, thoughts, attitudes, behaviors, and a narrative that reinforces how unfair it was that you were a person that was harmed, injured, or assaulted in an event that you believe was cruel, unfair, and out of your control. Essentially you develop a filter that twists everything to be interpreted by your mind with a theme that says *terrible things will always happen to me.*

And we know [with great confidence] that God [who is deeply concerned about us] causes all things to work together [as a plan] for good for those who love God, to those who are called according to His plan and purpose.

Romans 8:28 (AMP)

Now, look closely at that definition because the words *beliefs, thoughts, attitudes, and behaviors* are all attributes that create any mindset. So, my thinking is this—if you can have a successfully toxic, defeating mindset, then you can have a *victorious mindset* too. If you can be successful at one, you can be successful at the other because the fundamentals are all the same. We need time to recalibrate, learn, and execute, which requires focus, repetition, and effort. By the way, the victim mindset took focus, repetition, and effort to create too! So, you cannot doubt if you can do this because you already have done so, but it was more unintentional than this mindset will be. Just imagine what intentionally changing your mindset will do for you then!

While it may take time to change your thinking, by doing this with God as the center piece, things can happen quickly. Plus, He is in the redeeming business, so please don't fret about the time you have wasted because God can redeem it all!

It is so much easier to renew your mind when you understand some of the Spirits behind this way of thinking. We need to pull some weeds, plant some seeds in your mental real estate garden, and nurture those seeds into a prosperous, flourishing garden. It's like what the Lord says; you reap what you sow. Stop expecting to see strawberries grow from a dandelion seed.

The overall generic concept of a victim believes they are always adversely affected by a force or agent. And you wouldn't be entirely wrong because that force or agent is the principalities and rulers of darkness in this world. However, it's the intention and focus behind the mentality that becomes the true issue. First Peter 5:7 tells us that we have an adversary, the devil, working to devour us. However, Jesus won the war and rescued you when He died for you on the cross. If you can see that you are safe and nothing can harm you in Jesus, it will become easier for you to drop this belief system. Let me ask you if the most potent force in the world is for you, who can be against you (Romans 8:31)?

He canceled the record of the charges against us and took it away by nailing it to the cross. In this way, he disarmed the spiritual rulers and authorities. He shamed them publicly by his victory over them on the cross.
Colossians 2:14-15 (NLT)

It is a deep-rooted belief system that bad things will happen because one subjects him or herself to oppression, hardship, or mistreatment.[1] Since the belief is so deep-rooted, those with the victim mentality walk around with an attitude that shouts, *"Poor me or woe is me!"* Such people cannot take responsibility for their actions because they always find an excuse as to why they are not at fault and why it is someone or something else's fault. They believe people are always against them, and their unhappiness is everyone else's fault, which also says it is not their responsibility.

Individuals with a victim mentality demand and deeply desire rescuing yet are impossible to save due to all the walls and excuses they latch on to. Since they can only see life with a lens of oppression wrapped up in a *woe is me* outlook, they are consumed with negative thinking. During adversity or hardships, their first thought might be the fantasy of someone coming and saving them.

It was not until after I overcame this kind of victim thinking that I realized I had it. If I am offending you or you disagree with anything I am saying, I encourage you to ask the Father right now what is causing you to get offended or upset. You see, I allowed the words of my offenders to become real in my mind. What they said about me became what I told myself. Starting around

---

1 "Victim Mentality," 2019; "Definition of Victim," 2019.

age seven, my brother would say to me every day until about age sixteen, when I was dying from an eating disorder, that I was stupid, fat, and ugly. My brother constantly shamed me for how I looked and for not being a boy. Of course, I see the stupidity in it now. But, as a little girl who just lost her father, I saw him as a father figure, which made the words cut even deeper. I now know I should not have looked to him as a father figure, but I was seven and wanted a dad and a protector. If he was not telling me that I was stupid, fat, or ugly, my mom or people at my school were. I always imagined someone coming and rescuing me from the hell I was in, but no one came, and when I was offered an out, I held on to my comfort zone. I chose to stay.

Another common thread in the victim mindset is that they see all their life challenges as someone else's fault, even if they have zero proof.[2] Again, they lack responsibility for their actions. Victims place a higher amount of expectations on others. There is a basic level of expectations we unconsciously put on someone. However, a victim goes much further with that. Remember, sometimes anger at a person is an unfilled expectation that most likely was not communicated. So, it's fair to say victims may have some anger issues.

If any of the descriptions of a victim registered with you, note that you did not develop this thinking in a

---

2 Watzpatzkowski, 2016.

day. As you go through this book, pace yourself. Make small obtainable changes. I had a coach once who said, "I would prefer you to make one sustainable change a week because that's fifty-two changes a year." Slow and steady is how you will change your thinking. Pace yourself. Also, know you cannot do this in your own strength. It would be best if you allowed Jesus' yoke to come upon your neck. Self-will will not get you to freedom, but agreement with God will. Therefore, prayer will also be a significant portion of this process. Rely on God's strength, not your own. Never forget that you do have the same Spirit that raised Christ from the dead inside of you (Romans 8:11)! Allow the Holy Spirit to be your guide, comforter, and advocate. He will help you change far quicker than anyone or thing.

Then Jesus said, "Come to me, all of you who are weary and carry heavy burdens, and I will give you rest. Take my yoke upon you. Let me teach you, because I am humble and gentle at heart, and you will find rest for your souls. For my yoke is easy to bear, and the burden I give you is light."
Matthew 11:28-30 (NLT)

Prayer: Father God, I come to you asking for Your help, strength, and comfort. Please help me to renew my mind and to see how victorious I am in You! Would you please help me hear and know the promptings of the Holy Spirit when I want to quit or do anything that lines with a victor? Father, fill me with Your Spirit. Would You please teach me how to put on Jesus' yoke and not take it off? I do not know how to do this transformation, but I know You do. Would You please guide me and comfort me the entire time? I want Your will for my life, not my own. Thank You for Your everlasting love, grace, and forgiveness. Help me to grow in Your strength. In Jesus' name, amen.

CHAPTER 2

Victim to Victor!

Signs of a Victim Mentality

Maybe you are a bit like me, and you are unsure if something fits. If that's you, hopefully, examining a person's behaviors with a victim mentality will help you! The list that we will go through is very, very powerful. It enables you to put things in perspective and take your thinking to a higher level. Invite the Holy Spirit in right now to help you put all of this into perspective for you.

Prayer: Holy Spirit, I ask You to come into my heart and guide me. If I read anything that I am or have been doing, please convict me. Please open my spiritual eyes to some of my worldly and anti-Christ ways so I can become more like Jesus and less like my flesh. Thank You for convicting me of the victim mentality inside of me. Thank You for providing me with a revelation that will allow me to walk out of such ways and renew my mind to the Word of God. In Jesus' name, amen.

First, you will see a victim mindset behavior exemplified, followed by comparing how a victor may respond in the same situation. There are a handful of different scenarios I will explore to examine and contrast. While it may seem like the list will not end, it's essential you read them all. As it might help you get out of a similar situation or help you identify if you are participating with a victim mentality. In that case, you will know how to rely on the Holy Spirit, increase your thinking, and perhaps even respond differently than you typically do.

Helpless to Helpfully Proactive

An individual with a victim mindset sometimes feels powerless, unable to take action, solve the problem, or cope effectively. Many people with the victim mindset do not have healthy coping skills. When the victim mindset faces a huge problem, they typically give up, run away, or wallow in their reality. While the individual's feelings are real to them, it is not the truth. Believing you are helpless, cannot solve the problems you face, or cannot develop healthy coping skills are all lies that come from the enemy. One of the first things you must start to do is renew your mind to what God says and break the agreements you made with the enemy. If you want to admit it or not, that victim mindset did not come from the Father. If it did not come from our Heavenly Father and He is not for such thinking, it must come from the devil. Anything that is not of the Father is anti-Christ.

Now here is what a victor would do when facing a grim, challenging, and overwhelming situation. First, victors will pray because Peter tells us to cast all our worries on to God because He cares about us so much (1 Peter 5:7). After choosing to invite God into the situation through prayer, the victor will ask the Father what to do. Here's the thing God is all-knowing, and believe it or not, He knows the best way to handle this situation, and He will tell you. Now, you might have to take a leap of faith, but God will never leave you. Oh, and guess what? If you do make the wrong choice, God will reroute you just like a GPS does.

Victors want to identify where action can be taken, regardless of how small or large that step may be. God calls us to put our faith to work, and that is what a victor will do! Victors want to move forward.

Many people throughout the Bible boldly move forward by taking steps of faith in the face of fear! If you believe you must be free from fear before you move forward, you are quite mistaken. It is about allowing your faith to move you forward while keeping your focus on Christ. Here is the thing, by partnering with God and using your free will to agree with His Word, your faith will start to drive out your fear!

I encourage you to see this way as more of a solution-focused thinking pattern or mindset. Victors will not always be able to fix the situation, but they can move their focus away from a problematic way of thinking. Besides, when you obsess over the problem, you only agree with the kingdom of darkness, which will only lead you into more fear, overwhelm, and frustration. Here is an example of a solution-focused question:

How can I help myself move forward towards my goals? How can I change my perspective to view this situation as an opportunity for growth, not a tragedy? How can I look at this situation objectively, and what can I do about it? What can I learn from this situation? Where am I allowing my fear and emotions to hinder me from following God?

Exercise: Identifying My Obstacles

At some point in our life, we must deal with obstacles, problems, and setbacks. It's part of life, but obstacles, issues, and delays do not have to define you. Before we can begin to think like a victor, we must identify some of our most common life obstacles, problems, or setbacks.

Review your past and identify which past events or themes keep coming up and replaying in your mind. Typically, the events we allow to play on repeat in our minds are matters we have yet to overcome and are holding us back, causing us not entirely to be present.

Start to break down each problem one-by-one. Apply the following questions to one problem at a time:

- What events in your life do you view as traumatic, problematic, or stop you from moving forward?
- How does this event make you feel today? (Afraid, unworthy, anxious, etc.)
- What is another perspective that empowers you to change your approach?

For example, I was not particularly eager to fail. Then I realized failure is a gift as it helps me learn, and I enjoy learning. When I began seeing failure as an opportunity for feedback and a chance to recalibrate better, I was more open to putting myself in new situations that made me uncomfortable.

Over Exaggeration to Strategic Partnership

Another typical behavior that the victim mindset will do is exaggerate their problems. They see most of their issues and challenges as traumatic catastrophes. They act like every problem will be the death of them. They even may say statements like, *"it's going to kill me,"* or *"this will be the death of me."* Essentially the victim mindset blows everything out of proportion and accompanies everything with an excuse. It's the "drama queen" attitude or the "woe is me."

Whereas victors will be more objective to what they see and qualify as a genuine problem. Yes, they, too, will face hardships and suffering, as this is a promise in life. However, they will first give it to God and trust that God will somehow, someway redeem the situation or pray that He is glorified in the process. Now, please do not misunderstand as a victor can also buy into the enemy's lies and act with the woe is me attitude. What sets them apart is the time frame and their heart attitude. Victors do not want to stay in this oppressive mindset. When they do fall into the devil's trap, it is for a short period. Once they see they are in that frame of mind, they will talk to the Father about it, retrace their steps, identify when they bought the lie, and then talk with the Father on how they can be more aware of the devil's schemes.

When facing challenges, the victor asks, *"Where am I over exaggerating this problem? What does God say about this problem?"* Victors may also identify the worst-case scenario in an objective frame of mind instead of a fear-based one and make a short plan to respond if that happens. If the worst-case scenario occurs, what will my next move be? Victors tend to keep themselves focused on the truth, which is what God says about something. They are conscious when using their mental energy, playing out situations because they know they can either serve the kingdom of heaven through faith or the kingdom of darkness through fear. Since victors want to be proactive, they may choose to have a handful of options to pivot to if a worst-case scenario occurs. Another behavior that separates victors from the victims is how they use their mental energy. A victor will practice self-control by implementing thought-control, keeping their eyes focused on Jesus, and not meditating on what they do not want to happen.

"So then faith comes by hearing, and
hearing by the word of God"
(Romans 10:17, NKJV).

Everyone's Against Me to Trusting the Lord

Another common thinking pattern in the victim mindset is the belief that most people are against them. When they meet someone new or offer to help them, they may first think the worst. Believing that the person has a secret agenda, doesn't want to be their friend, but wants to destroy them. It's paranoid thinking that everyone is out to get them. They struggle to let people into their inner world. They may believe compliments have ulterior motives. It's an underserving kind of thinking. They don't deserve beautiful things or caring people because clearly, they are not valuable or worthy. Sometimes, this way of thinking is due to the individual's past experiences where they have experientially learned they cannot trust people.

"It is better to take refuge in the Lord than to trust people"
(Psalm 118:8, NLT).

One of the most significant differences between the victim's mindset and that of a victor is that victors put their safety, security, and trust in the hands of the Lord, not humans. A victor allows the Father to validate, affirm, encourage, and empower them. Through their relationship with the Lord, it becomes more attainable for them to love all and separate the sin from the person.

A victor accepts compliments. Even if the praise comes from an individual with ulterior motives, victors know that it is not their problem and that they can only implement their control where they genuinely have it. Victors see that they cannot change anyone. They rest on the truth that only the Holy Spirit can. They give everything up to the Lord. When people set out to hurt them, instead of responding in retaliation, they will pray to the Father for that person's heart, love them, and be a blessing to them.

Victors want to encourage and point all to the Father. They learn how to give and bless others with compliments, as well. They see individuals who cannot accept compliments as insecure, ungrateful, uncomfortable, or prideful towards someone trying to bless them. As for those compliments, victors see kind words as a verbal gift or blessing. It's not about them agreeing with the compliment as much as it is about openly accepting a gift from someone else.

I was like this too. I remember it was difficult for me to accept and even give compliments. Until I chose to see compliments as a verbal gift. It was then that I realized someone was trying to bless me, and I was refusing the blessing. Who was I to disagree with other perspectives about something they liked, appreciated, or were pleased to see? I began to ask the Father, "How can I accept kind words over me?" I encourage you to ask the same as well. Where do you struggle to believe people may see you in a kind, warm light? What is making you think that compliment is not sincere?

For me, the answer was because someone very close to me hurt me and lied to me constantly as a child. I was allowing the pain they inflicted upon me to steal moments of joy brought to me by others—I was projecting my pain of the past onto innocent people. Once again, the devil was at work.

Exercise: Acts of Kindness

Acts of kindness are powerful both for the doer and the receiver. One way I encourage you to start normalizing compliments and praise is by giving them, but please make sure they are genuine. This week try and do two of these, but make sure your heart has pure intentions. After you have done an act of kindness, write about how it made you feel in your journal. Below are a few ideas:

1. Buy a stranger a cup of coffee.	6. Pay the toll for the car behind you.
2. Buy a homeless person a meal.	7. Buy the food for the car behind you in the drive-through.
3. Leave flowers/candy at someone's desk or at their house.	8. Send a random house your favorite book.
4. Cook someone a meal.	9. Babysit for free for a mom/dad in need.
5. Send someone a card telling them how much they mean to you.	10. Return shopping carts that have been abandoned in parking spots.

Changing the Perspective on Hardships

Victims think they are the only ones suffering and in pain. What a lie, and do you see the extreme self-righteousness in this way of thinking? Everything is about them and about why their life is awful and why they cannot move forward. It's the woe is me mentality accompanied with excuses, self-obsession, and focusing on the problems! The victim mindset sees every tragedy or setback as a curse from God. The story of Job shows his friends doing the same.

Victors have a different perspective on hardships and trials. James 1:12 says,

---

Blessed [happy, spiritually prosperous, favored by God] is the man who is steadfast under trial and perseveres when tempted; for when he has passed the test and been approved, he will receive the [victor's] crown of life which the Lord has promised to those who love Him.

James 1:12 (AMP)

Just as James is saying in the verse above, victors know that trials and suffering can be the means through which the Father's blessings will come. Instead of hyper-focusing on the issues at hand, they keep their eyes locked on Lord Jesus, who has overcome the world!

Look at Jesus! He went through profound suffering, persecution, and trials, and look at the blessing that came out of that! Victors understand that their endurance to stand in and victoriously overcome a difficulty can bring God's blessing to fruition. Since they are convicted to stand firm in the face of trials, suffering, and even persecution, they do not try to seek avenues of escape. Still, they boldly move forward, trusting God is with them. The Father uses trials, suffering, and hardship to help His children mature emotionally and spiritually in situations.

Victors understand that as long as they are on earth, they will face hardships, and therefore so will everyone else. However, the comfort of this reality is not brought to them by the fact that others will suffer but by the truth that Jesus' peace is with them. They remember that it is through their weakness that God's power is made strong. Victors take comfort knowing that whatever they face, God's grace will get them through it. Notice the perspective shift. Victors are not relying on their own strength but the power within them through the Holy Spirit. Additionally, James also tells us in this verse that God will not leave you in that place. He will provide a way for you to escape if the testing becomes unbearable.

No temptation [regardless of its source] has overtaken or enticed you that is not common to human experience [nor is any temptation unusual or beyond human resistance]; but God is faithful [to His word—He is compassionate and trustworthy], and He will not let you be tempted beyond your ability [to resist], but along with the temptation He [has in the past and is now and] will [always] provide the way out as well, so that you will be able to endure it [without yielding, and will overcome temptation with joy].

1 Corinthians 10:13 (AMP)

Perhaps you do not understand why God even allows for His children to go through trials. He tells us His reason in the Mosaic Law in Deuteronomy 8:16 (AMP), which says, "That He might humble you [by dependence on Him] and that He might test you, to do good [things for you at the end." It can be easy for someone to take delight in their own prosperity and become proud that their hard work and cleverness made them rich, but that's not the truth. Such thinking makes it easier to push God out of your life, and God wants to always be in a relationship with you. It is God who gives one everything they have. Therefore, God will ask you to manage it for Him humbly.

All of this is excellent news for you too! If you are struggling with any of these victim ways of thinking. If one person can overcome their traumas by successfully surrendering them to God, so can you! Delight yourself in this truth. There is tremendous hope that you can walk out of the bondage too with Lord Jesus. Imagine what you would be doing with all that extra time and bandwidth you will gain when you walk out of some of these thought patterns. You must help yourself too, and one way you can do that is by doing the work to renew your mind, which can mean many things—for example, reading the Word of God every day—putting into practice what you learn. Catching your mind sending you false thoughts or beliefs and intentionally redirecting your mind to the new thought. I encourage you to ask the Father how He wants you to go about this too. He needs to be invited into all your decisions.

Reframing the Narrative

The story or narrative the victim mindset focuses on is mostly around being that—a victim. You see, victims hold on to the stories and emotions, which caused them to believe they are a victim. They shut down other people's perspectives and opinions regarding their problems and past traumas. They will even shut down what God has to say about something.

Whereas victors identify the repetitive stories, they tell themselves and then reframe that story. There is usually more than one way to look at something, and sometimes you have to choose to see things in a different light. When you can see things in a ray of acceptance, mercy, grace, and forgiveness, your world can quickly transform for the better.

I encourage you to find ways to reframe the narrative that may be holding you back. Try writing down what you are telling yourself about something and dig deep. Be honest with yourself. You may be lying to yourself about an experience in your past, which may be keeping you in bondage. As you think about that narrative you need to let go, I encourage you to:

1. *Identify what and how this story provides you with some sort of significance?*

2. *What significance does it make you feel?*

3. *Do you enjoy the negative, stunned reactions of the people to whom you tell the traumas too? If not, what is it? If you're not sure, ask God to show you if there is any twisted enjoyment you're holding on to.*

4. *What enjoyment or pleasure are you getting from reliving the wounds and not letting them go? If you don't know how to let them go, have you talked to the Father about it? He wants to take it from you, but you have to make up your mind to surrender it to Him and keep surrendering it back to Him every time you choose to take it back from Him.*

5. *How do you want to be seen? What story do you need to tell yourself to be seen this way?*

For many years, I, too, struggled with keeping a negative, self-destructive narrative on repeat. I did not know how to even reframe the narrative at first. I didn't see the narrative I was telling myself as harmful to me. Please know I am not encouraging you to lie to yourself. Instead, I am encouraging you to see things from different angles. I allowed the narrative I told myself to control and keep me in an oppressive and fear-filled state of mind. When I finally got honest with myself and was willing to face the truth that perhaps there was more than one narrative about what I endured, I got released from that destructive narrative.

I learned that I got some twisted enjoyment when telling people what I endured as a kid. It felt like I was being confirmed that my childhood was, in fact, quite abusive because I was confused if what I went through indeed happened or not, let alone if it was normal or not. I also was confused if that was abuse or even if I was being *dramatic* about it all. It also helped build a sense of self-worth, as I had none back then. I felt good, strong, and capable when I shared with them all the emotional, sexual, physical, and verbal abuse I had gone through. It was a reminder that said, *"Yeah, I went through that and am still here today—look at me."* When the better narrative needed to point to the Father! The truth was I was not present in my life or even feeling very capable. My past traumas consumed me. I felt mentally tortured and did not know how to escape.

I struggled to accept my reality (both past and present), and I kept looking for people to affirm my past when only God could do that. The reality was I liked the reactions I got from people because their stunned faces, to me, justified the crazy abuse and trauma I had endured. Do you see how I was looking to humans instead of God?

But I hated my quality of life. So, I changed my narrative. My narrative still focused on the hardship I had faced, but I saw it in a light of true strength and trust in God. I had endured it, and I could become bitter or better, and bitter was not working out for me.

I focused my thoughts and told my mind what I was going to think about, and I trusted God to redeem my past and use it for His glory. Essentially, I broke up with that narrative, and every time it came back, I would focus on my new narrative and then praise the Father!

Part of this is wanting God's will for your life more than your own will. I finally got to a point where I had tried everything that the world says to do. I went to therapists, after therapists, and none of them would take away the pain in my heart. When every therapist wouldn't get me to the freedom, I found myself even more frustrated. However, I believed the freedom I was searching for was possible.

Nonetheless, after the last therapist failed me, meaning that did not get me to where I wanted to be. I went and earned my own degree in psychology. That is where God truly met me. In my degree, I learned that psychology did not have the answers and that most of psychology, at least positive psychology, comes from spiritual ideas, but without the power of God. It was then and there that I decided to try it God's way. What did I have to lose anyway?

God can take everything and turn it into His glory if you allow Him to. Additionally, I also changed my agenda. At an unconscious level, I always sought to share my woe is me story with people because I enjoyed seeing the shock on their faces. Once I realized I needed to change my narrative, I also noticed I had to change my life's mission. Instead of wanting to be saved by a human, I gave my entire life to the Father. It was not an easy journey, but God was with me every step of the way. All I did was continued to keep seeking, asking, and knocking for Him in everything.

Keep on asking, and you will receive what you ask for. Keep on seeking, and you will find. Keep on knocking, and the door will be opened to you. For everyone who asks, receives. Everyone who seeks, finds. And to everyone who knocks, the door will be opened.
Matthew 7:7-8 (NLT)

Additionally, I decided to stop sharing the story of my past. I no longer talked about my past traumas to people. I validated my trauma and chose to start living life. I finally realized that there was never going to be enough validation. Even if my abusers confirmed my perspective, it was not going to take away the pain. The only thing I could do was give it all to the Father, so I did. I did this by switching my focus from me to helping people and doing God's will in my life, and there were many times where I was not sure what God's will would be for my life. However, I never gave up the pursuit, and God kept revealing His will for my life. Stay on the journey. He does have you, even if you do not feel He does. Let your faith be bigger than your fears!

Exercise: My Ideal Self

Imagine a world where time is irrelevant. You have all the time, skills, and resources in the world. Whatever you can imagine, you have. Describe your ideal self in a perfect world. Use your senses (sight, taste, touch, smell, and hearing) to describe this world. Who would you be? What would you do? How would you talk? How would greet people? Where do you live? What is your profession? What is your lifestyle? What is your mindset? Are you married? Do you have kids? Describe who you are and what your ideal self is! Once you have it down on paper, find ways to work towards those attributes.

Letting Go of the Past

As mentioned in the previous section, the victim mindset wants to hold on to the past. Unfortunately, holding on to the past is not good enough for this way of thinking. Instead, the mindset wants to continue replaying and reliving those painful memories. What happens is that the victim finds it hard to forgive, becomes easily angry at the world, and is hungry for revenge. Sometimes they do not care who falls victim to their wake.

However, victors choose to forget the past and forgive the person. We will discuss more about forgiveness in a later chapter, but here is a little tasting of what is to come about forgiveness. When victors interact with the people who may have inflicted pain on them, they forgive their persecutors. To forgive essentially means you have chosen to free the person from the mental jail you are keeping them in. You give up the right ever to bring up that hurtful event again. Here is the thing forgiveness is a choice. Yes, your mind will want to replay the painful events, but you must decide to practice thought control, discipline, and talk to that memory. Tell it to go in the name of Jesus! Meditating on the affliction will not help you, I promise! Victors understand they cannot fully forgive if they do not choose to stop thinking about the adverse event.

A victor understands we all fall short, and since we freely receive grace, compassion, mercy, and forgiveness from our Father in heaven, we should also freely give that to others.

"If you forgive those who sin against you, your heavenly Father will forgive you. But if you refuse to forgive others, your Father will not forgive your sins"
(Matthew 6:14-15, NLT).

Victims have conditioned their minds to think a certain way for years. The neural pathways that they continually choose to walk on each day grow stronger and stronger, which is why victors decide to renew their minds. It might take time, but when you do it God's way, time is obsolete. At some point, you have to say enough is enough and try a completely different approach!

There is a technique that neuropsychologist sometimes uses in dealing with PTSD in patients. It's an exercise that helps suffocate the neurons that lead to that memory. Here is what you do. Imagine you are in a physical location, like a house, store, barn, or something with tangible objects that you can use as checkpoints. Every time that negative memory comes up, choose to see yourself a step or two further away from the main object.[3] Keep taking steps back, and eventually, you will no longer recall the memory.

For example, there were many times where my brother would strangle me from behind. Usually, he would do this out of the blue when I got to the front seat of my mom's car before he did. To help paint the scene, my mom would always park her vehicle in the garage. When that memory would come back to my mind, I would see myself outside of the car. Then when it would come again, I would take a step back. When it would come again, I would take more steps back until finally, I was out of the garage. I would keep taking giant steps

3 Leaf, 2013.

back until the memories dissolved. Now, I still remember these things when I consciously think about them, like I just did. Do they hurt? Of course, but I see them differently. Now, when I reflect on who my brother was then, I see the pain, evil, and sin in my brother. I now know how to separate the sin from the person and love the person regardless. Love is very powerful!

Another technique used to break obsessive thinking or calm yourself down when your brain might register you are in danger or even when you are struggling to stop thinking on that thought is to scream, *I have joy, yes, I do. I am joyful; yes, I am. Joy. Joy. Joy. Joy is mine through the Lord!* I know this sounds silly, but it will work.

Saying that will break the loop of the memory in repeat. Then after screaming the phrase, think of some of your favorite memories where you felt a tremendous amount of love or connection. Choose to direct your mind to all the memories that bring you joy. What this does is it will release oxytocin in your brain. Like I said above, love is very powerful, and oxytocin is referred to as the "love" hormone and neurotransmitter, and it will cut through that loop. Don't believe me? Then try it out next time you are struggling! *Pause here, write down that joy phrase, and identify some memories you can consciously think on when you are struggling with fear or the victim mindset.* The reality is the battle will come; the question is, are you going to be prepared?

The past is in the past. What can you do today to help yourself move forward?

Many victims want the people who have hurt them to suffer. However, forgiveness is powerful and liberating. Please remember you need to forgive yourself too. Have you forgiven yourself? Sometimes, individuals who have endured lots of pain struggle to forgive themselves for having to endure such hardships. In a chapter to come, we will discuss ways you can practice acceptance and move past the discomfort of your past reality. Work on acceptance. Accepting things as they are and focus on things you can change within yourself.

Quitting May Not Be the Answer!

When times get tough, victims give up! A victim naturally focuses and finds problems. Rarely do people hear solutions out of a victim's mouth. Instead, one hears problems, why it won't work, and how it cannot work. They make excuses. The victim mindset doesn't want to participate in the displeasure and discomfort of working hard to achieve something when they believe they are not confident enough for it to happen, so they stop even if it's a high value of theirs.

On the other hand, victors see every challenge and obstacle aiding to their growth and victory in Christ Jesus. Victors have a strong foundation of resiliency embedded into their belief systems. Instead of finding reasons for why they cannot do something, they find all the reasons why they can achieve it, assuming it's God's will for their life. The Bible is a great place to start identifying the truth about your potential.

Dancing with Internal Conflict

The victim mindset creates division, destruction, and war within a person. Most individuals who have a victim mindset either have low or lack self-esteem. The victim mindset causes the person to believe they are unworthy, incapable, and can only do what others think they can do. That is exactly what self-esteem refers to because an inner sense of worth allows a person to be resilient, resist attacks, and digest criticism better. Ultimately this internal dance and tension within them cause them to be against themselves and even others. The conflict battling inside them can cause them not to trust themselves, which is known as self-doubt. When you combine low self-esteem with self-doubt, it is pretty easy to fall upon self-hatred. That low self-esteem can result from not liking themselves, which unfortunately causes a person to be quite insecure and even prideful, or as the Lord calls it, self-righteous.

Of course, it might not be easy for the individual to see that they are controlled by the words of others versus their own convictions. Since others' beliefs and opinions influence them, they will typically not do what they want. Sometimes they are even afraid of their own shadow.

When I was in my late teens to my early twenties, I had a strong victim mindset. If you didn't know me and looked at me, you might not know, though. I could walk into a room and own it, but I had zero self-esteem. Please do not confuse self-confidence with self-esteem. It is possible to be confident in oneself but not have any esteem, and vice versa. I will discuss this more in the chapters to come.

However, a victor knows their worth, and they do not rely on themselves or what others say for it to be cultivated. What victors understand that the victim mindset fails to comprehend is that they know how loved they are by the Father. They know that He is greater than they are. How could you not love yourself when the holiest, greatest, and most loving thing in the world says, "I love you!" You see, where the victim mindset fears man, the victor fears God. Now, this fear is one of respect, loyalty, and a yearning to be obedient. One could say it is a healthy fear. Like the child-parent relationship.

Victors understand that they are not better than almighty God. Victors trust the truth, not their own opinion. Nor do they believe their opinion is greater than God's. When the Father says something, the victor chooses to accept and believe it, regardless of their opinion about it. Yes, there may be a walking it out period, meaning the victor might have to walk it out with the Father until the revelation comes from the Holy Spirit, but nonetheless, the victor chooses to hold on to the words God says, not that of man.

"Fearing people is a dangerous trap,
but trusting the LORD means safety"
(Proverbs 29:25, NLT).

Unfortunately, there is a lie that is saturating planet earth. It is the principle of "self." While you may think I am contradicting myself, understand I am not. Yes, I am saying words like self-esteem, self-doubt, and self-hatred, but only because humans have titled it. I want you to focus more on the heart attitude and intention behind the difference. The victim mindset screams to the individual that they are a god unto themselves, which unconsciously will make them believe they are in opposition to God. When one is in opposition with the Father, they will deny His statement of love and open themselves up even more to the enemy. Ultimately, they agree with the enemy and disagree with the Father. It's foolishness, but let's be honest—the world screams self this and that! The reality is that the kingdom of self comes from the devil. The victor replaces "self" with Jesus!

The other large discrepancy between the victim and the victor is that victors choose to build themselves up and celebrate everything. Their expectations are reasonable and achievable. They adopt a grateful attitude, not a complaining one. Victors celebrate even their small wins.

"Be thankful in all circumstances, for this is God's will for you who belong to Christ Jesus"
(1 Thessalonians 5:18, NLT).

Now part of this transformation will focus on developing a foundational level of self-esteem, self-confidence, self-belief, and resiliency through Jesus that will allow you to move forward regardless of what happens. You must understand that God has you. Now, the life you think you want and the life God wants you to have might not line up. Here's the thing, what God has in store for you is way better than anything you can imagine. Choose to follow Him and do life His way, and your world will change. As you follow Him, your desires will become His desires! You will want to do what He wants you to do!

The Deep Root of the Spirit of Fear

The victim mindset comes from two deeply rooted and interconnected spirits that are a part of the kingdom of darkness. One is the Spirit of Fear (*I capitalize Fear because it is an entity*), and the other is the Unloving

Spirit. The Spirit of Fear breaks down into a handful of sub spirits that all link back to the Spirit of Fear. However, it appears, Fear of man (*seeing man as their god and not trusting God*) and Fear of rejection (*fearing man rejecting them as opposed to God*) are quite intense in the victim mindset. Fear of man and Fear of rejection allows them to be controlled by others and creates division inside themselves. Fear of man will quickly rob a person of the peace that God intended for us to have. Now Fear of rejection causes a person to draw back from people, lie to people, and not open up to others because they are afraid of being rejected. Fear of rejection tells the person who they are is dependent on what others say about them. Whereas that Unloving Spirit tells the victim mindset that you are unacceptable and unloved by God. It's important to note that one can very much struggle with both these entities and not have a victim mindset.

Here is how that victim mindset can play out. Those with a victim mindset will quickly change their opinions to what others believe to not feel rejected. There is a belief in them that is reinforced by the kingdom of darkness inside of them that causes them to believe others know more than they do. The victim mindset causes people to become followers of anything. Since they cannot stand up for themselves, they will sometimes blame others for their choices. Additionally, Fear of man accompanied by the Fear of rejection can cause a person to become a people pleaser. The victim mindset says one has to buy people's approval.

A victor may not be completely free from the Spirit of Fear or the Unloving Spirit. They may be walking it out with the Lord. However, the biggest difference is the awareness piece. Victors have a strong foundation in the Lord and know how to use discernment and the sword of the spirit to fight off these spirits. In part, victors are also hungry and willing to walk with the Lord because they understand it is God's perfect love that will drive out all the Fear.

"There is no fear in love; but perfect love casts out fear, because fear involves torment. But he who fears has not been made perfect in love"
(1 John 4:18, NKJV).

Victors trust in the Lord with all their heart and do not lean on their own understanding (Proverbs 3:5-6). Since they trust in the Lord with all their heart, they are better at implementing and upholding their boundaries. They know when they need to say "no," when to speak up, and when to keep quiet. One could say the victor has grown both emotionally and spiritually mature. Unlike the victim, the victor chooses to let the Lord justify their worth and belonging.

Exercise: Here is an exercise you can write down and contemplate. Identify five scenarios in your life where you chose to please people instead of making your own life decisions. How did this affect you? What was the result of such a scenario? What do you wish would have happened? If you had done what you wanted, where would you be now? What have you learned from this? When someone else disagrees with your decision, how will you stay committed to following through on the decision? What's the overall theme you have learned from allowing others to take control of your life? How can you care to do what God says over man?

Toxic Thinking to Operating in the Mind of Christ

The thoughts of the victim mindset are negative, foolish, prideful, toxic, and ultimately cause the individuals to sabotage their lives. Neuroscience has proven that we work to create our most dominant thoughts! The Bible also tells us this information. As a man thinks in his heart, so he is (Proverbs 23:7, NKJV).

The victim mindset allows the imposter or inner critic to dictate their life. They stop moving forward when they hear that imposter or inner critic. Now, if we are honest, those thoughts are coming from an anti-Christ spirit. Additionally, the victim mentality allows their emotions and feelings to control them, which causes them to settle for less than they want or could have if they chose to agree with Lord Jesus. In fact, at times, those possessing a victim mindset will be dishonest with others and themselves because there is too much pain for them to accept or even tell the truth.

Whereas victors take every thought captive and bring their thoughts into the obedience of Jesus Christ, as Apostle Paul says in 2 Corinthians 10:5. What that means is victors take that anti-Christ thought in their head, capture it, and talk back to it, letting that thought know what God says about the matter. They speak the truth, God's Word, to all thoughts that go against God's Word. It is pretty hard to identify an anti-Christ thought, let alone teach those thoughts to obey Christ if you do not know what the Word of God says about the matter, which is why it is so important to read your Bible. Another reason why victors take their thoughts captive is that they understand the power of their thoughts and words. Proverbs 18:21 tells us that life and death are in the power of the tongue! Victors also choose to think on the following eight general thought topics as Paul writes in Philippians 4:8: things that are true, honest, just, pure, lovely, admirable, anything worthy of excellence and praise.

And now, dear brothers and sisters, one final thing. Fix your
thoughts on what is true, and honorable, and right, and pure,
and lovely, and admirable. Think about things that are excel-
lent and worthy of praise.
Philippians 4:8 (NLT)

The Catch-22

Have you ever come across a person whose norm was to complain about how no one would help them, and then when someone asked if they could, the person wouldn't accept the help? That may be the victim mindset. They are notorious for complaining only not to accept help! Most of the time, the victim mindset becomes quite busy with people-pleasing that they make sure everyone else is happy and omit their own needs. They exhaust themselves by pleasing everyone else, refusing to ask for help until they are burned out and drained. The victim mindset believes asking people for help is a sign of weakness.

A victor identifies when they need to rest. They take care of themselves first because they understand if, by failing to prioritize their needs, they can only help someone but so much.

Contemplate: Where are you overextending yourself? What are your fears regarding stopping? What is the truth about these fears? What does self-love look like? How can you set healthy boundaries?

Lacking Grace

The victim mindset inflicts self-punishment when they believe they have "messed up." They do this by attacking themselves with blame, pity, and punishment if things do not go their way or a way that they see as wrong. Victims tend to become self-destructive when things go wrong. They ultimately lack optimism, grace, hope, faith, and resilience. Instead, they partner with the "who cares mentality," choosing to make things worse.

Victors participate in providing themselves with compassion, kindness, mindfulness, and forgiveness through the lens of Lord Jesus. When victors make a poor decision (which will happen), they pray, repent, and practice solution-focused thinking to find a strategy. They spend time reflecting on their choices by asking, *"What should I have done? How can I do this tomorrow or the next time this comes up?"* Victors are about forward movement, moving towards God's will, not allowing anything to knock them down. Of course, there will be plenty of times where they get knocked down. Again, it's the heart attitude of the victor, which encourages them to get back up and continue trying. Victors spend time reflecting on what motivated them to choose that choice and how to prevent making the same decision again. Essentially, they know they are not perfect and give themselves grace when they "mess up." Victors understand it is not about perfection but growth, and even the slightest step forward is a win and needs to be celebrated!

The Taste of Bitterness

The victim mentality struggles with deep bitterness and does not know how to forgive, practice self-control, or love unconditionally. Ultimately, they do not know how to give grace. Bitterness comes about when one chooses to continually brew on how unfair it was that someone wronged them or hurt them. They brew due to unresolved anger, which creates bitterness, producing deep hostility and anger. Those who hold on to bitterness do not understand that it destroys them, not the one they are upset at. Bitterness consists of seven spirits: unforgiveness, resentment, retaliation, anger, hatred, violence, and murder.

The spirit of bitterness is progressive until the person agreeing with the spirit chooses to cut it off through the power of Lord Jesus. First, the victim mindset holds on to a record of wrongs, which is known as unforgiveness. Next, resentment accompanied by the desire to get even comes about inside of them. Then the victim mindset becomes angry at the individual who wronged them, leading them to hate the person and ultimately start imagining or behaving violently towards the offender. Finally, the bittered person falls on murdering the one they are angry at, and please understand murder can come through the tongue! Jesus makes it quite clear that His followers are not to repay evil with evil, and even imagining something that is against the Father's commands is the equivalent of doing the act!

Instead of forgiving the offender, the victim mindset has nurtured and grown the pain, hurt, sorrow, and anger of the event, until the tragedy of what happened to them has contaminated their thinking and life. Bitterness destroys life. The Word of God tells us not to seek revenge but to surrender our pains to Him and trust that God will avenge the wrong. The only way to remove bitterness is through forgiveness. Holding on to past wounds does not hurt the offender but the person choosing to hold on!

Now victors are quick to forgive, pray for their enemies, separate the sin from the person, and love unconditionally. Victors understand who their real enemy is, and it is not flesh and blood.

For we are not fighting against flesh-and-blood enemies, but against evil rulers and authorities of the unseen world, against mighty powers in this dark world, and against evil spirits in the heavenly places.
Ephesians 6:12 (NLT)

Additionally, victors do not see a person who has chosen to do an evil act towards another as evil. They understand that one action does not make a person evil or not. Giving grace to others is part of the victors' makeup because they know humans make mistakes.

The Father does not stop loving someone simply because they sinned, does He? No! The Father separated the sinful act the person chose to agree with from the action or behavior. Essentially, our Heavenly Father looks past our flaws, looks past the evil and sin, and still chooses to love the individual. This is what the victor does too! Please understand God does not want you to sin, and He will not bless sin.

Benefits of the Victim Mentality

The fact of the matter is we do not typically do anything unless there is a benefit to it, fleshly speaking. The things that we do in life provide value, regardless of if it makes logical sense or not. Most likely, if you are struggling with the victim mentality, you are mainly operating out of your carnal mind instead of the mind of Christ, which requires you to see with your spiritual eyes.

For those who are living according to the flesh set their minds on the things of the flesh [which gratify the body], but those who are living according to the Spirit, [set their minds on] the

things of the Spirit [His will and purpose]. Now the mind of
the flesh is death [both now and forever—because it pursues
sin]; but the mind of the Spirit is life and peace [the spiritual
well-being that comes from walking with God—both now
and forever]; the mind of the flesh [with its sinful pursuits] is
actively hostile to God. It does not submit itself to God's law,
since it cannot, and those who are in the flesh [living a life that
caters to sinful appetites and impulses] cannot please God.

Romans 8:5-8 (AMP)

We continue to participate in such behavior because
it satisfies a need we believe we have. The actions are
giving us something—even if that something is negative. There is some reward or benefit that we see that
continues to drive that behavior. Please understand the
brain can get miswired, sending you false signals. Here
are some of the advantages of living with a victim mentality. Notice benefits do not give life or align to the Father's will.

- Not taking responsibility.
- Practicing avoidance, which feels better than
  facing their fears or problems. However, avoid-
  ance leads to more suffering.
- Chronic complaining can lead to attention.
- Negative attention is received, and negative at-
  tention is still attention.
- Less likely to be criticized.

- A sense of control is created as others may feel compelled to help you.
- Drama occupies their time and distracts them from pursuing goals.

Notice most of the things listed were all things that one must handle spiritually. Psychology cannot do what only God can do. I am not saying therapy, counseling, and psychology cannot help you. I am merely saying that the supernatural power of the Father cannot be missing from the equation. There are times where both will come into play, but ultimately, it is the supernatural power of God that makes all things possible, not psychology.

Prayer: Father God, I want to live for You, not for me. I want to grow into the mind of Christ, and I want Your will to be done in my life. Please help me to see when I am rejecting the mind of Christ and Your will. Give me Your desires and take away all the desires that are not in alignment with Your will for my life. Father, raise me up to be a victor in Christ! Thank You for Your love, mercy, and grace. In Jesus' name, amen!

CHAPTER 3

How Is a Victim Mindset Created?

Have you wondered what causes one person to go woe me, while another doesn't complain or wallow in self-pity at all? Sure, a person's childhood has a huge hand in it, but I wanted to specifically know what made it more difficult for some compared to others. I hated how I would wallow in self-pity. I wanted to be brave, fearless, and courageous, but for some reason, I would usually give up. Then I learned about soul wounds, and I began having a greater understanding of myself. For me, understanding the engineering of something helps me to put the principles into action. I hope this chapter helps you too!

The creation of the victim mindset comes to play in many ways but usually stems from what the parents teach their kids, what kids see, abuse, trauma *(an incident that is mentally scarring)*, or exposure to death at a young age name a few. It's easy to fall prey to victim thinking, especially when exposed to hardships or soul wounds at a young age. In this chapter, I want to explain to you what soul wounds are, provide some common scenarios that help instill the victim mentality, and explain how all this can impact your future relationships.

Soul Wounds

A soul wound occurs when you need or expect a loved one (child, parent, spouse, sibling, grandparent, or caretaker) to be there for you and then discover that your loved one was absent in a time of need. In our minds, we magnify the pain of this event because society tells us we are to count on these people, and they will never reject us. If that loved one remains unavailable or hurtful in other ways, the injury and pain of that event sear our souls.[4] People who sometimes adopt the victim mentality have constantly endured soul wounds from the ones they were closest to. Interestingly, the people who say they love us the most sometimes become our greatest source of pain, injuring our souls the greatest. Over time, it becomes normal for the wounded to protect themselves from such individuals by developing a relationship style to aid in their protection until they choose a more excellent way. The more excellent way is God's way!

---

4 Clinton & Sibcy, 2006.

Of course, this is slightly bittersweet. While the wounded is hurt by the person closest to them, they also yearn for love and acceptance from the caregiver or family member too. Sometimes a lost person will do anything to receive love from another person.

Believing You Have to Be Ill

It can be astonishing what a person will do to feel loved. Another reason why we develop a victim mindset is because we create a paradigm, and the results satisfy a need, in spite of that resulting in being healthy or not. For example, a child who develops a victim mindset to survive may want love and attention. But they learn they can only get love and attention by pretending to be sick, behaving as weak, dramatic, angry, or allowing bad things to happen. Typically, humans only do things that fulfill a need or bring value. Remember, that value can be harmful. For example, a toxic relationship is still a relationship. Sometimes the fear of changing their ways, also known as Fear of discomfort, keeps them in the habit of doing what is already normal and comfortable. Additionally, sometimes people learn to play the victim because of what they watched someone else do. Some people never outgrow or stop thinking with a victim mindset. It is normal for one to believe what they were taught as a child.

Did any adults around you constantly complain about the people who wronged them? What influential people in your world participated with any of the signs of a victim mentality? If so, you may have emulated their behaviors because it provided a way to gain personal power and attention. Besides, it is normal for young children to copy what they see.

A Codependent Parent

Another cause for the formation of the victim mindset comes through the codependent relationship with a parent. Children can become burdened and feel responsible for their parents' wellbeing, either taking care of them mentally or physically or believing they oversee their happiness.[5] Or maybe it was a way to survive their childhood and get their needs met. Children require attention and love. When it's not offered or readily available by their caregivers, they are left to find other ways to receive it.[6]

An Abusive Childhood

Another reason comes from suffering abuse as a child. All abuse wounds a child's soul and spirit. You want to talk about a soul wound! When a child experiences sexual abuse, it can plant the weeds for shame

---

5 Watzpatzkowski, 2016.

6 Watzpatzkowski, 2016.

to develop. In turn, this can then cause the individual to grow up with no self-esteem. They may feel they are responsible, and they identify their self-worth with sex.

I know this is what happened to me. The first blow to my self-esteem was my dad's sudden death two months after my seventh birthday. In case you do not know, fathers have a huge role in developing a child's self-esteem. After he passed, I endured physical, sexual, psychological, and emotional abuse as a child. One minute my family was more whole and provided much loved. The second minute my family offered false hope, and the love became more like a roller-coaster ride. It was a push-pull dynamic. For me, sexual abuse began off and on around age seven or eight and lasted for a handful of years. I remember around seventeen, I began to associate my worth in life with having sex with people I didn't want to have sex with. At age fifteen, I aesthetically transformed. I looked older than I was, I acted more mature than I was for my age, and it became normal for older adult men to hit on me. Trust me; I know how that sounds! Like many men and women out there, I, too, continuously heard messages that said I was not good enough, smart enough, or capable of anything but sex! Those messages became normalized to me over both direct and indirect feedback. To make matters worse, I did not receive sexual abuse from just one man but many.

One of my abusers was only ever kind to me when he was sexually abusing me, and when I would tell adults, they would say to me what I experienced was normal. No, it wasn't! Since I received this message a handful of times, I stopped telling adults when I was experiencing sexual abuse because I figured it was normal or what I had to do. But, for me, I was so used to men taking advantage of me and other adults telling me they weren't taking advantage of me that I associated my self-worth with sex. I felt an obligation to have sex, or men would be mean to me. Thankfully, through the love of Christ, I broke that thinking. If you have the same kind of thinking, please know you can break it too. You need to learn a more excellent way, which I hope this book will help you find through Lord Jesus! If you have not heard it lately, please know you are worth far more than sex. You are special. You are the apple of God's eye. Through Christ, you are strong, powerful, and can do all things through Him who gives you strength! You are more than enough. You are loved!

Deficiency Language

Lastly, the language used in a home can create a victim mindset too. "Deficiency language has created a world of description that understands only through what is wrong, broken, absent, or insufficient."[7] Essen-

7 Kollar, 2011, p. 26.

tially it is when a child only hears what they do wrong and how bad they are. The home lacks grace, love, forgiveness, and encouragement. Unfortunately, sometimes parents can make you feel you have to earn love by doing well in life as opposed to freely giving unconditional love.

If all you hear is how bad you are, then you will become that. We become what we think. When you are speaking deficiency, you speak from the Spirit of Fear and, more specifically, the Fear of poverty, extreme self-hatred, perfectionism, with a deep root that love is earned. The belief there is never enough. Such a mindset of focusing and speaking all that is going wrong with your life, omitting room or the focus of finding a solution—leaves out the possibility for hope and overlooks God's power to work in your life. Deficiency language sucks you up like a black hole. The language of faith is missing in the individual. The language of faith is composed of love, hope, positive thinking, and the conviction that all things are possible with God.

"Don't use foul or abusive language. Let everything you say be good and helpful, so that your words will be an encouragement to those who hear them"
(Ephesians 4:29, NLT).

I share all this information and insight around a victim mindset to showcase how it came about inside you. I hope this information helped you gain more understanding and hopefully help you walk out of some of your unhealthy ways. Perhaps you noticed it all came from the kingdom of darkness. Please remember you were made in God's image! God is love! Your true home is in the kingdom of God!

I hope you can see how sneaky the enemy is and how quickly he will devour a person. It doesn't matter how old they are, as he is ruthless. He wants to destroy you the second you come into this world. Praise God that Jesus has overcome the world, and it is through Him that we are victorious. It's time to break up with that demonic way of thinking and start to see yourself as a victor.

Here's the most incredible thing. Since the victim mindset is learned, you can unlearn it! It's my opinion and my experience that the fastest way to unlearn something that comes from the kingdom of darkness is by using the sword of the spirit, which is scripture and God's way. I will talk more about how to do this in a later chapter. The question comes down to how willing are you going to be to do the work that falls in your control? God wants you to help yourself too! You have to do some work too, and He will not bless sin!

Everything I will share in this book is what I did to help break the chains of the victim mindset inside of me. Again, a big part of this is leaning on Jesus and learning the Word of God. I am a living testament to this. If I can unlearn all of this and stand as a victor, or what I like to call myself—a Warrior for Christ—then you can too! I eagerly want to help you become a Warrior for Christ!

Here is how I see it. First, one has to walk as a victor before they can be a Warrior for Christ. I say that because one has to have a strong foundation of knowledge, skills, and trust before becoming a successful Warrior for Christ. There is a sanctification period that has to occur, and not everyone is willing to go through it. Just as God needs to know He can trust and rely on you to move forward amid oppression or suffering, you also need to trust Him with your life. Learning how to trust the Father can take time. I encourage you to focus on one day at a time and even one step at a time too. Think of it this way. In the military, it takes time to move up in rank. Depending on how quickly you hone your skills, focus, mindset, and commitment to your branch will aid in your advancement to move up in position. Rarely if ever, do you see an untrained solider enter war! Once you have a strong foundation in God, continue asking Him to grow you and equip you to be a Warrior for Christ. The way I explain a Warrior for Christ is an individual who is 100 percent focused on doing God's will for their life, understands spiritual warfare, and is willing to die for Christ. They trust God entirely. Love the Lord with all their heart, soul, and mind (Matthew 22:37) and are hungry to live righteously no matter the cost. Warriors know who their real enemy is and excels in spiritual warfare. They are tough, resilient, and willing to go where the Lord takes them.

Additionally, Warriors work consciously to overcome all their fears to help advance the kingdom of God. They courageously share the gospel wherever they go and strive to operate out of the mind of Christ and be more like Christ in everything they do. When Warriors get knocked down, they quickly get back up and are ready to go back into action. They are willing to lay down their life for another and diligently work to uphold God's commands in all they do.

Warriors for Christ require a keen focus. One needs a robust knowledge of the Word of God as this enables them to do the godly thing in any situation. Warriors are hungry to exemplify Christ wherever they go. God will help build you, prepare you, and guide you. All you have to do is have a willingness to be used in His kingdom and remain obedient in all that He asks of you. He looks for a willing heart. Do you have a willing heart to be all that God wants you to be?

Invite God into every aspect of this process. He will guide you. You are not alone. You can transform your mind because the Word of God says you can!

But first and most importantly seek (aim at, strive after) His kingdom and His righteousness [His way of doing and being right—the attitude and character of God], and all these things will be given to you also.

Matthew 6:33 (AMP)

CHAPTER 4

Attachment Theory

Some people believe birth is the first trauma a person experiences. Think about it. You go from an environment where you have everything you need, like food, warmth, protection, security, safety, and constant connection, to being ripped out and alone. Then you may grow up experiencing soul wounds or unhealthy behaviors that can quickly capture your future.

Attachment theory is a fairly large and complex psychological theory. However, for the purpose of this book, I have boiled it down to the most foundational elements. There are four kinds of relationship styles that we fall into based on how we were raised as children and experienced as babies. Your relationship style will either be an anxious, avoidant, disorganized, or secure. Based on the kind of relationship style you have will depend on how well you think like a victor or a victim. It may be important to highlight that the anxious, avoidant, and disorganized relationship styles are all saturated with the Spirit of Fear and the Unloving Spirit.

Regardless of how your relationship style is currently, understand you are not destined to stay there. As followers of Jesus Christ, we have authority in Him and have the power to operate in His mind. It takes time, spiritual maturity, and dedication, but all things are possible with God!

The Anxious Relationship Style

The anxious relationship style is based on a thought process of fear, more specifically, the Fear of abandonment. The Fear of abandonment is a deep belief that others and God will abandon you. The only way you can break this belief system and the agreement with the Spirit of Fear is by understanding God will never abandon you. Having the revelation that you are accepted, adored, and loved by God is key here. Ask the Holy Spirit to make this truth real to you!

Those with an anxious relationship style tend to feel a sense of incompetence, low self-confidence, and hunger for strong protection. Typically, they are anxious, and other times they are melodramatic and may have some ignored anger within them.[8] Usually, these people are a product of an emotional confusing home. Perhaps there was lack of stability, performance love,

_____
8 Clinton & Sibcy, 2006.

absent parent, or inconsistencies in emotions. Emotional confusion is where one moment the person they love gives them a reason to think they are so important, but a moment later, the beloved person makes them feel unimportant. It's that push-pull scenario. They experience a yin and yang relationship, which begins to corrode their core beliefs about their ability to be loved and to get the love they want and need. The belief that can be cultivated in this kind of environment is the belief that one must succeed to receive love. What one must remember real love is freely given. Those with this relationship style begin thinking, "I have to please my loves, or I'll be worthless and unlovable." Unfortunately, this belief system leads one to believe they cannot give love nor be loved.

People with anxious relationship styles have a belief system that says:

- I'm not worthy of love.
- I'm incapable of getting love without getting angry, clingy, or desperate.
- Others can meet my needs but might not do so due to my flaws.
- Others can be trustworthy and reliable, but they might abandon me because of my worthlessness.

In a nutshell, the anxious relationship style tends to have great Fear of abandonment, Fear of rejection, and Fear of poverty, causing them to go to great lengths to please people. The cool thing is God can break all this inside of you!

The Avoidant Relationship Style

Now, the avoidant individual is also greatly impacted by the Spirit of Fear as well. However, they typically fear: Fear of intimacy, Fear of man, Fear of failure, Fear of abandonment, Fear of rejection, and lack of self-esteem. They struggle to trust people and firmly believe one must only rely on themself, leading them to be highly independent individuals. When they do not receive the autonomy they desire, they may feel trapped, causing them to lash out with anger or pushes people away. The avoidant relationship struggles with emotional connection, sharing private thoughts and feelings, and are uncomfortable with touch. The behavioral style of this relationship is a bit narcissistic, disconnected, or compulsively perfectionistic. By the way, perfectionistic thinking is very destructive. It causes a person to believe they can be a god, believing that they can do everything, be everywhere, and know everything all at once. Some struggle with addiction, and ironically, many of them are angry with God.

The Disorganized Relationship Style

The disorganized relationship style is greatly affected by dissociated pain, a shattered sense of self, untold stories of an unresolved past, and a compulsion to repeat painful past experiences. These individuals also tend to show traits of both the anxious and avoidant relationship styles. They are pessimistic, always seeing darkness before the light, and almost exude negative thinking.

Disorganized relationship individuals believe they are unworthy of love. They think they are incapable of getting the love they need without reacting with anger or being clingy. They have this absolute way of thinking where no one is trustworthy and how everyone is abusive. Sometimes they think they deserved what they went through. The disorganized struggles to trust people, highly suspicious, and also suffers from Fear of abandonment. Sometimes they can be extremely uncomfortable with the reality of love but may feel more comfortable fantasizing about it.

The Secure Relationship Style

Whereas the secure relationship style is comfortable with their humanity and can easily express emotions and vulnerability. These individuals create a healthy dynamic of dependence and independence within the relationship, appreciating the truth they can rely on one another. The secure relationship style builds their relationship on honesty, trust, communication, forgiveness, understanding, and emotional closeness. Such individuals also thrive on their own as they do not depend on another human's approval. The very healthy, secure relationship puts their trust and security in Christ, not in humans, which allows for a more mature relationship to occur. Sense such individuals have security in the Most High, it is easier for them to fight healthily, instill appropriate boundaries, can negative interpersonal issues with ease, and be more positive about their relationships.

Let's check in; which relationship style most resonated with you?

Father God, I want to be a healthy person. I see where I have bought lies instead of the truth. Please forgive. Father, help me to put down my unhealthy ways and pick up Your life-giving ways. I know I do not allow you to be my absolute security, and I don't like it. Please help me to put my entire trust, worth, and security in You and no one else. In Jesus' name, amen!

CHAPTER 5

The Victor Mindset

Okay, enough about that victim mindset. Let's talk about living as a victor in Christ Jesus! While reviewing the victim mindset elements is helpful, it is more vital we spend our time discussing and explaining how to be and live victoriously through Christ Jesus.

What Is the Victor Mindset?

Like I said previously, the victor mindset is the foundation for you to continue building upon. The list I am about to go through is in no particular order. It is more about the traits and behaviors that help aid this mindset. I encourage you to identify the ones that may be easier and more challenging for you to develop. Look for ways you can start incorporating these attributes into your daily life. Also, focus on taking small bite-size steps towards this way of living. Smooth is steady, and steady is smooth.

Let's pray!

Father God, as I read through these lists of traits and behaviors regarding the victor mindset, I ask You to highlight all the ones that I can start implementing into my daily life today. Holy Spirit, please bring me a revelation. Please help me see where I am and am not living to honor You and exemplify Christ. Thank You for enlightening and opening my spiritual eyes of understanding, highlighting the fleshly and worldly ways that I have been living. Give me the strength and desire to live only as You would have me live. If I get overwhelmed, send me Your peace and remind me that I can do this as it is Your will for me to live for You! In Jesus' name, amen.

The Attributes of the Victor Mindset

1. Victors live with connection, knowing and believing they are loved and worthy! They know they are *more* than enough. Victors understand how much the Father loves them through having the revelation that they are loved, important, and capable by the Father.

2. Victors have a prosperous, growth-minded mindset. They focus on doing good, living by Christ's values, and understanding that it is faith that pleases the Father. Victors concentrate on their efforts and work to change their hearts with the help of the Father. It is not about the victor being naturally skilled but putting their

faith to work to develop the skill sets and Christ-like traits. Essentially, victors are persistent. They do not rely on their own skills, capabilities, or self-will but on the guidance, wisdom, and truth of Lord Jesus.

"Let us not grow weary or become discouraged in doing good, for at the proper time we will reap, if we do not give in" (Galatians 6:9, AMP).

---

3. Victors refrain from placing unspoken and even spoken expectations on people. They understand that unfulfilled expectations lead to anger and take responsibility when they find themselves in such a predicament. Therefore, victors communicate effectively and put their entire trust in the Lord. They do not look for man to affirm them or take care of them. While God uses people to carry out His will, victors understand that if a human falls short or may not be obedient to the promptings of the Holy Spirit, that they can rest in the truth that God can redeem all things.

4. Victors are strong and courageous. They take to heart what Joshua 1:9 (NLT) says, "This is my command—be strong and courageous! Do not be afraid or discouraged. For the LORD your God is with you wherever you go"—understanding that the worst thing that can happen to them is still a win. It is just like Paul wrote in Phi-

lippians 1:21 (KJV), "To live is Christ and to die is gain." Therefore, victors comprehend the truth that they have the Lord's strength at their disposal and, through their authority in Christ, can overcome anything.

5. Victors understand the power of faith. Just as muscles must be worked out for them to grow and develop, so does faith. Therefore, victors are focused on growing and developing their faith muscles. While there is very little we can do in our own strength, victors are continuously in prayer with the Father. They live by faith and not by sight. Victors understand that through their faith in trusting Jesus, they are made children of God, and since victors hunger to be children of God, they are led by the Spirit of God.

Now faith is the assurance (title deed, confirmation) of things hoped for (divinely guaranteed), and the evidence of things not seen [the conviction of their reality—faith comprehends as fact what cannot be experienced by the physical senses].
Hebrews 11:1 (AMP)

---

6. Victors understand the power of thoughts and words. They realize their life is created by what they think and diligently work to take all the disobedient thoughts to Christ's teaching into captivity. Additionally, they are conscious of what they speak, doing

their best with the Father's help to refrain from speaking death, but only life. Victors understand that it is through their words that their faith and authority in Christ are released.

7. Victors spend time disciplining their flesh and learning to control their emotions. Instead of doing what feels good, they live to do what is righteous. They understand their works will not save them. Victors spend time doing what is right in the eyes of the Father because of their love for Him. They understand their emotions can sometimes be wrong due to a miswiring in their brain. Therefore, instead of willingly accepting and agreeing with every emotional sensation throughout their body, they hold it with curiosity and exploration. While they may fall into reacting at times, their focus is learning to grow and mature from such incidents and find ways to respond better that resemble Christ.

For God did not give us a spirit of timidity or cowardice or fear, but [He has given us a spirit] of power and of love and of sound judgment and personal discipline [abilities that result in a calm, well-balanced mind and self-control].
2 Timothy 1:7 (AMP)

---

8. Victors know their mind can either control them, or they can control their mind. Many psychologists out

their believe humans cannot control what they think. While many thoughts can come from external stimuli, it is up to you to latch on or tell them to go in the name of Jesus. The Bible makes it very clear that we can control our thinking! The theme of Jesus' first sermon was to change your mind, explaining what it looks like to live as His follower and be a part of God's kingdom. Jesus encouraged people to focus on the kingdom of heaven and not think about gratifying the fleshly desires. Additionally, there are many verses throughout the Bible that articulates God did give and wants us to use our sound mind, which means self-discipline. Only the world encourages a helpless, woe is me way of living.

The Benefits of a Victor Mindset

You can probably already see that there are some tremendous benefits to living with the victor mindset. Below is a shortlist of some of the benefits of renewing your mind to God's Word.

- Increased self-confidence as you will look to God, not to man or yourself, to affirm you.
- Believing in your heart that with God, nothing is impossible.
- Increased resilience.
- Trust the Father to be their supply of joy, strength, and hope.

- Think on positive, life-promoting things as we see in Philippians 4:8.
- Respond with and operates in the mind of Christ.
- Allow the peace of God into their heart. They have peace of mind.
- Live in the present.
- When life gives them lemons, they make sweet lemonade, and not just for themselves. They are grateful, and it shows.
- Emotionally mature. They own their mistakes and take responsibility for any of their negative, inappropriate, or unhealthy behaviors.
- Their focus enhances because they live for God and do what they are told.
- Anxiety, worry, and stress do not consume them because they put their trust in the Father.

CHAPTER 6

Shame and Guilt

For many suffering from the victim mentality, shame and guilt can rule their being. However, shame and guilt can also appear to be the same thing, but they are not. Sometimes it can be helpful to learn how to label your emotions as this can naturally create distance from the sensations. Doing this can be difficult when you are not clear on which is which. I hope that this chapter helps you better understand shame and guilt while also finding a way to break up with it.

Shame

Maybe you are walking through life with a sensation of shame. Perhaps you feel shameful for even feeling shame, but please know shame is universally experienced. I do not think there is a person on this planet who hasn't felt shame. Even Jesus endured our shame on the cross, and He despised the shame. Jesus deserved to be honored, praised, and adored. Instead, He received public humiliation, dishonor, cursing, and ultimately shame.

Shame goes back to the beginning of time too. Adam and Eve felt shame! After Adam and Eve sinned by eating the forbidden fruit, man fell. However, the result of their sin left them with a sense of shame and fear. By eating the fruit, Adam and Eve's eyes were opened to good and evil. What this means is their consciousness was awakened. They understood good and evil, both like and unlike the Father. For the first time, Adam and Eve realized they were naked, which made them feel embarrassed. Genesis 2:25 stated they were naked and felt no shame, but they felt shame immediately after their eyes were opened. What did they do to save and protect themselves? They made aprons out of fig leaves to cover themselves, which exemplifies they were trying to save themselves through empty works. Some of us do that today! Where we rely on our works to save us instead of our faith in Christ!

Adam and Eve did not only feel shame, but they also felt guilt. Shame and guilt can coexist together. Shame caused them to be embarrassed about being naked. The guilt they felt caused Adam and Eve to hide, as guilty feelings can make a person hide. The result of man's fall due to Adam and Eve's choices is that most humans are afraid of God today. We can rejoice because Jesus has disregarded our shame. You must keep your eyes on

Him and not on anything else. Jesus is the author and finisher of our faith. Look to Him and not to man.

The enemy has been selling shame lies from the beginning of time, but Jesus stopped it. Some people walk around not knowing this truth, though. At some point, you must choose who you can believe: God or the devil. Even Adam and Eve doubted God's faith and put more trust in the enemy. Jesus has proven and shown us that we can trust God and must not trust the devil. Stop buying his lies.

Shame is twisted. Remember, the devil perverts and twists things. Many people feel shame about things that might seem super silly to the outsider. Shame can affect all of us, especially when we make man or society our god.

Shame limits us and causes us to live behind a façade preventing us from operating as our authentic self, which is only found in Christ Jesus.

Participating with the thoughts of shame is a waste of time because Jesus pays no attention to it. He already redeemed it. Stop choosing to agree with it. Jesus has already paid the ultimate price.

Admittedly it has been a while since I have felt a deep sense of shame. However, this was not always the case. I used to feel shame about a lot of things, but as I strive to be still and know that He is God, He has taken my sensation of shame away. It's incredible what you will quickly walk out of when you do things the way Jesus says. I remember that shame would make me feel terrible about myself and consume me, causing me to focus on myself, which means I took my eyes off Jesus. When I allowed shame to destroy me, my mindset was on a lack. I was focusing on how I was not good enough when again, Jesus says I am. He says you are too!

I began spending all my mental bandwidth on beating myself up, which would only produce self-rejection and ultimately self-hatred inside of me. Additionally, the shame caused me to detour away from Jesus' and my values.

When you allow the past to consume you because you are holding on to unforgiveness and lacking grace or mercy, how can you move forward with God's will for your life? I cannot focus on my agenda when shame is screaming in my ear. You must see the freedom and authority you have gained in Christ so you can break the agreement of shaming yourself. Some are doing a better job destroying themselves that they leave no room for the enemy to attack. Stop beating yourself up! You are forgiven and free from condemnation. Now, no, that does not give you an excuse or a reason to continue sinning. The Father wants your heart to be open, soft, tender, and desire the things He desires for you. It's about changing your heart to align with what God says, and He says you are forgiven. Now, if you do mess up or experience something shameful, give it to God. It is really that simple and that difficult all at once.

What Is Shame

What exactly is shame in the emotional context?

Shame is an emotional response to a failure, shortcoming, or other wrongdoing regarding what society expects or what a person expects of him or herself.[9] The Bible defines shame as disgrace. Again, if you follow Christ, you will never be put to shame. Shame can make a person feel unworthy of connection, which may come from having a deep desire and hope to leave a situation or never see a particular person again. Ultimately, shame comes out of the Fear of rejection. Someone has made you feel rejected for something you did or for something done to you. Since shame makes one feel rejected, it may cause one to feel disconnected from their peers or society. Remember, nothing can separate you from the Father. He is with you. He will not forsake you nor leave you. Now, you can reject Him, but He will accept you back with open arms! At some point, you may need to be clear on what connection is most important to you. The connection that the world brings or that the Father brings. You cannot serve two masters. I say this because when you realize that you are affirmed, loved, adored, appreciated, and secure in Christ Jesus, noth-

---

9 Ungvarsky, 2019.

ing and no one can take that away from you. In fact, having a strong relationship with Christ is one way you can build your treasure in heaven. People and things will come and go, but Jesus will never leave you! You can leave Him, but He will not leave you!

Shame can create a deep feeling that you are too unworthy of connection because you have not lived up to an expectation or goal. What a lie! If you feel this way, please understand that your works do not save you. It is your faith in Christ that saves you. Perhaps it is time to reevaluate your expectations and goals. Are they even realistic? Or are they idealistic, causing you to chase a fantasy?

One of the best ways you can break shame is through understanding the power of God's love, mercy, and forgiveness. You must start learning how to forgive yourself quickly and realize that you are a human being. I will shed more light on this in a chapter to come. You will fail a handful of times because you are not God. When you ask for God to forgive you, you are quickly forgiven. It becomes water under the bridge, and He too wants you to move forward.

If you have thoughts like "I'm not good enough," "I'm unworthy," or "I'm unlovable," then you might be battling shame. It's time that you get clear on the truth because God says you are more than enough, worthy, and loveable.

While you renew your mind, shame might keep telling you that you are flawed, and it may feel excruciating. You have to understand none of it is true. Why? Well, why would God say that you are the apple of His eye (Psalm 17:8) if He felt like you were flawed?

Part of breaking these chains means you want freedom more than bondage. You are going to have to make your mind up and get intentional. When the shame gremlin comes shouting into your head, talk back to it. Tell that gremlin to go because you are the apple of His eye!

For You formed my innermost parts;
You knit me [together] in my mother's womb.
I will give thanks and praise to You, for I am fearfully and
wonderfully made;
Wonderful are Your works,
And my soul knows it very well.
Psalm 139:13-14 (AMP)

Shame is rooted in fear, and Jesus conquered fear! Focus on what Jesus says, not what your feelings, friends, or parents say. Again, you *can* do *all* things through Christ Jesus!

Let's get a head start on the enemy. There are a handful of places that are more common for one to experience shame. For instance: body image, appearance, money, work, parenthood, family, mental health, physical health, addiction, sex, growing older, religion, surviving trauma, and any place where another person may stereotype or label you! Take a few seconds to identify where you most experience shame and identify a verse that you can recite to that shame gremlin when it comes knocking on your mental door.

Once you experience shame, then what happens? Many things can come up. For instance, you may start to protect yourself by blaming someone else, rationalizing what happened, giving empty apologies, or hiding. Notice that Adam also did those. In Genesis 3:12, Adam blames Eve in front of God. Then Eve responds by blaming the serpent. Of course, the blame game happened after the two tried to hide from God. Unfortunately, the blame game is a waste of time! If it won't work for Adam and Eve, it won't work for you either. Stop going there. Take accountability, repent, and accept God's forgiveness, mercy, grace, and love.

While you will not like, agree with, or appreciate every decision you make, you must learn how to take accountability for your choices. Nonetheless, not taking responsibility for your actions is foolishness. God gave you free will, and how you choose to use your free will falls on you. It's pointless to participate in the blame game as it solves nothing. Additionally, it's silly to hide from God as He is omnipresent, omniscient, and omnipotent. Instead of deflecting, blaming someone else, or trying to run from God, turn to Him. Ask for His strength. Ask for His forgiveness. Ask for His help. Ask Him to show you how He sees the situation and how you can learn from it! Even ask Him to redeem it!

Background of Shame

Shame is usually first experienced when we are children, either by our parents, caregivers, or teachers. Children do not innately know how to shame someone until they experience shame. Children who experience intentional or unintentional rejection from someone they hope to receive attention from will have a sense of unworthiness. Another way children experience shame is when they are scolded for something continuously—something they have no control over. For instance, children need to learn to control their emotions. Unfortunately, parents do not always want to teach their kids how to do so. Instead, they will shame the child for the emotion or sensation they are feeling. There is a time and place to discipline a child, but it is never appropriate to discipline the emotion. Effective discipline occurs when the parent punishes the behavior, not the emotion.

Physical and sexual abuse will also lead to the development of shame. I can attest to this. I remember feeling just like I was this horrible, unworthy, and useless person. I had to work to restore a healthy relationship in a few areas where shame was king. Jesus helped me see Him as King over my life, not shame!

Maybe you are wondering what causes shame to even come about inside a person? Psychology believes shame occurs due to humans desiring the need for human approval. *Reread that one more time, please.* Notice the human does not desire God's approval, but human approval. I am not saying it is unhealthy for a human to want to fit in or belong. I am simply saying it is dangerous for a human to fear humans more than God. We are to look to Jesus in everything, not to man, things, or other idols. Jesus is always the answer!

"Dear friends, don't be afraid of those who want to kill your body; they cannot do any more to you after that"
(Luke 12:4, NLT).

Notice how the enemy sneaks in here. When you feel another person disapproves of you, shame is the result. For this to occur, you must care more about what that person says about you than Christ. Therefore, part of breaking shame and walking out of the victim mindset is programing our minds not to hunger for human approval but to trust in our heavenly Father and work to develop a sound spiritual lifestyle and relationship with

God. It can take time trusting God, but you have to start somewhere! So, why not now?

Shame vs. Guilt

Now, let's examine shame in comparison to guilt. Again, learning how to label your emotions can aid in successfully navigating them. Shame and guilt have similarities, but that's it. The two sensations are different.

One significant difference between the two is guilt is typically tied to a specific event that contains intentional behavior. In contrast, shame is a result of an all-encompassing event caused by unintentional actions or no action. Shame says, "I am bad," whereas guilt says, "I did something bad."

There is nothing positive or helpful about shame; it is destructive. Now guilt, on the other hand, can be positive. The fruit of guilt can be a positive influence on your life.

Here are a few situations that demonstrate what shame is in comparison to guilt.

One may feel shame if they are bankrupt from not managing their money correctly. However, guilt in this example is when you spend money on something you did not need, could not afford, and later realized was a foolish decision to purchase. If you have ever bought something and later felt buyer's remorse, then you were experiencing guilt.

A second example of shame is if a manager calls you names or speaks down to you in front of your colleagues. Guilt may come over you after you have called a client the incorrect name.

Guilt

Guilt causes you to feel remorseful about something. Have you ever just felt awful about something you did, and all you wanted to do was make it right, or at the very least apologize? If so, that is an example of guilt. When you feel responsible for causing harm to someone or not treating someone as kind as you could have, guilt may be the fruit of it.

Ultimately, guilt helps a person to seek restitution. Guilt will lead a person to repent too. However, there are two types of guilt. Yes, that is right. The enemy twisted guilt too! Remember, the enemy is the author of confusion.

The two kinds of guilt are true guilt and false guilt. True guilt gets stirred up inside of you after you have sinned. I think most know that sensation quite well. Imagine if you didn't feel guilty after sinning. How could the Father redirect you or help you see you were in error? The Father uses true guilt to bring us into repentance. Please don't think guilt is a bad or wrong feeling.

When you feel guilt, you must explore it with the Father's help because the second type of guilt is false guilt.

False guilt is self-created. It creates self-condemnation for no reason other than you failed to live up to your own or someone else's expectations. Now false guilt can also result from holding on to unresolved past regrets and faulty thought patterns.

The sensation of false guilt can also be a result of obsessive thinking. If you find yourself feeling guilty but have not done anything morally wrong or sinful, it is most likely coming from a deep sense of unworthiness rooted in a person's childhood. It is easy to idolize your parents, adults, and even siblings and friends as children, forgetting that they, too, are human beings with their own spiritual problems, past bondage, and pain. As children, when we are blamed, punished, or humiliated for things we have no control over, this can create an extreme feeling of unworthiness. God uses people to carry out His will, but so does the enemy.

As a young girl, starting around age eight or so, my brother would tell me almost daily that I was fat, stupid, and ugly. As those words fell over me, brainwashing me, I began to believe him. As I grew older, my brother would continue to attack my stomach and my breasts, always making me feel a sense of disgust and contempt about my body. Unconsciously, I must have decided to care about my looks obsessively. Around middle school,

I started only wearing sweatshirts to school, no matter the temperature out. I grew up in the south, where humidity is ridiculously high, but I wore sweatshirts to hide myself and my stomach. I felt shame, guilt, and repulsion for my body. Who wouldn't, after hearing such hatred spoken over them day in and out?

Perhaps you can relate to this. Maybe kids or your loved ones made fun of you for something that was not entirely in your control. When this occurs, there is room for both shame and guilt to develop. Do you know what cuts those branches off from you? Jesus!

Notice true guilt focuses on God, and false guilt focuses on yourself or humans. Anything that stops you from trusting and obeying the Father, causing you to start to walk in your flesh instead of your spirit, is anti-Christ and not from God. A large part of the believer's walk comes down to intention, the heart attitude, and where you are putting your focus and trust!

Here is the tricky part. False guilt can have sin somewhere deep underneath it. To help identify if your guilt is true or false, get curious with the Holy Spirit's help. The Holy Spirit will convict you and help you discern the type of guilt you sense. The easiest way to determine if it is false or true guilt is by asking: Have I done something sinful? Am I regretting a past choice? Have I failed to live up to another person's expectations? Do I owe anyone an apology for what I chose to do?

If it is true guilt. Repent to the Father. Apologize to any individuals involved and even apologize to yourself. Ultimately, choose to take responsibility and be proactive about it, and the guilt will dissipate. Again, confessing your wrongdoings to God, the offended, and yourself can have a tremendous impact on releasing that sensation of guilt.

Combating Shame and Guilt

I hope you better understand shame and guilt. However, there is still a question to answer. *How do you combat shame and guilt?* The overarching answer is through Jesus, but there are a handful of strategies you can implement additionally.

First off, most therapists understand the danger of continuing to participate with unresolved shame and guilt. It can keep you in bondage and prevent you from living a healthy lifestyle. Personally, in my practice, I have noticed those who struggle with shame and guilt find it harder to break up with the Spirit of Fear, creating additional challenges in establishing healthy relationships.

First off, the Bible emphasizes and encourages reflection, analysis, and growing your awareness about your thoughts, past choices, and how you are currently making decisions. Secondly, God wants you to confess, repent, and forgive as He has forgiven you. I would even argue these qualities are the staple to cultivating a good spiritual relationship with the Father. It will help you develop a heart attitude that is pleasing to Him. When you have a strong relationship with the Father, it is easier to have healthy relationships with humans.

If we claim we have no sin, we are only fooling ourselves and not living in the truth. But if we confess our sins to him, he is faithful and just to forgive us our sins and to cleanse us from all wickedness. If we claim we have not sinned, we are calling God a liar and showing that his word has no place in our hearts.
1 John 1:8-10 (NLT)

Now that we have clarified the spiritual foundation and components necessary to break shame and guilt, let's turn our attention to some of the tactile strategies you can use. Here I will focus on what you can do to start to renew your mind in this area, allowing you to break the thought patterns and retrain your mind to a more excellent way.

We must learn how to move from shame to compassion while allowing our faith to come through, creating hope. When you begin self-shaming or feeling shame, ask yourself, is that how you would want your child, spouse, or best friend to treat themselves? Of course not. So, if we reversed the roles and this was someone you loved who was participating in cruel shaming self-talk, what would you tell them?

It is key to remember that shame wants to remain in the darkness. You will have to bring it out and expose it to light. Doing so will require some resilience on your part and consciously changing your internal dialogue. It's not about achieving perfection. It's about continuing to get back up even after you have fallen or bought the lies. Shame wants to live in secrecy. However, when you reveal that secret and even talk it out, you can begin to see how foolish or flawed the shame beliefs may be.

The only way we can combat fear is through faith and operating out of love. Both fear and faith project into the future. Fear is what you do not want to see in the future, and faith is what you hope to see.

Sometimes when we allow things to remain in the darkness, it becomes quite uncomfortable and unpleasant to face. It is human nature to want to avoid anything and everything that creates discomfort. You can even fear discomfort or pain. However, you will have to face these parts of yourself. When you face these uncomfortable parts of yourself, it can be easy to judge, criticize, or hate yourself, which is why you must practice mindfulness. While I will talk more about mindfulness in a later chapter, it is important to observe these uncomfortable thoughts mindfully. Doing so means you are observing and being curious about these thoughts, choosing to refrain from judgment. If you find yourself too afraid or uncomfortable to face these thoughts, call out to God. The more you rely on His strength and not your own, the quicker you will grow your faith.

I promise He can do things for you that you are unable to do without Him. There are few things I can promise, but that is one of them. When you try to become your own healer, protector, teacher, or anything else, you fall short. The reality is God wants to take all your shame, pain, sickness, and anything else that is not of Him from you. The only question is, are you going to let Him?

Now, if you are not ready to grow your relationship with God, that's okay. He is quite a gentleman. Take your time. What you will learn in time is without God, you will keep running into walls. Not to scare you, but you are on the clock. You will not live forever. Therefore, the sooner you make this decision, the sooner your life will transform for the better.

As you begin to change your internal talk, resiliently move forward, exposing the shame and guilt in your life, you will also need to identify your triggers. What causes you to agree with shame or guilt?

Maybe you are not even aware of what causes you to feel shame or guilt. We first want to learn how to become physically and cognitively aware of shame. What triggers you to feel shame? Just think about that question. As you contemplate that question, write down all the things coming into your head.

The second thing we must do is practice critical awareness. First, identify a shame or guilt memory that you want to analyze. Next, honestly, kindly, and accurately analyze the event. Would you please consider your actions and how others may have viewed them? From here, if you realize you did do something wrong or of poor taste—own up to it. Apologize to those involved, including yourself and God, and move on. If you need help objectively reviewing the memory, then perhaps these questions will help you as they did me. (1) Is what I am being accused of or accusing myself true? (2) Who said it? (3) Is this person's opinion any value or benefit to me? (4) Is the person honest or a prejudiced critic?[10] (5) How would Jesus navigate this situation?

You will not be able to do this in every situation, but it's a great place to begin distancing yourself from shame or guilt. These questions can also help you create separation from other people's cruel words.

Another thing you can do is flip the message. *Can you reverse the message and meaning of what is driving your shame?* For example, I used to struggle with body shaming myself when I overate. One way I flip my self-message is by acknowledging if I worked out that day or not. If I worked out, then I reminded myself the extra calo-

---

10 Peale, 1961, p.57.

ries are not going to hurt me. I also reminded myself that I do work out consistently, and one day of overeating will not destroy my progress. Then I would turn objective, telling myself that there was no way I ate an additional three thousand five hundred calories. You see, sometimes I would overdramatize the fact that I overate by acting like if I was going to gain five pounds due to it. Whereas the truth is for me to have even gained a pound, I would have had to eat my required amount of calories plus an additional three thousand five hundred more calories to gain weight. I stayed honest, objective, and proactive.

Additionally, I would remind myself that this shame is not coming from me but from darkness who wants to keep me paralyzed and controlled by not feeling good enough. Let's be honest for a second. Some days those thoughts are entirely consuming and relentless. When this occurs, I distract myself. While you might think it is avoidance, it is not. Functional distraction can be powerful when applied appropriately. Plus, unlike avoidance, functional distraction acknowledges you need a time out from the matter and will come back as soon as you are in an appropriate headspace. Typically, I would go on a walk, journal, call a friend, or do something to get me in the present moment.

Remember, shame likes to keep you in secret. That is what fear does. It wants to keep you in the dark, but if you allow yourself, the best thing you can do in these moments where isolation or secrecy is calling you, reach out to a close and trusted loved one. Even to this day, there are plenty of times where I call one of my spiritual elders to help save me from spiraling. While this does not happen often, it does happen. God tells us that man should not be alone (Genesis 2:18). We need one another.

Another thing you can do is start sharing the stories you feel shame about with those you trust and in a safe environment. *Are you owning and sharing your own story?* When you share the shameful experience, you put light on the event and a fresh set of eyes who can help you find empathy and self-compassion. Also, this individual may help you find a new perspective and narrative for the experience. Learning how to reframe things is very, very powerful. Sometimes there is more than one way to see something.

We now can relate the emotional reaction of shame mostly, not always, to a feeling of unworthiness. Therefore, worthiness is the key to freedom. Isn't the feeling of worthiness also a feeling of love? Worthiness means being good enough. You are good enough for love! Guess what? There are a handful of verses that say how much God loves you. Every one of you deserves to give and receive unconditional love. When you are loved perfectly, and when you receive that love, fear will leave.

> *And may you have the power to understand, as all*
> *God's people should, how wide, how long, how high,*
> *and how deep his love is. May you experience the love of*
> *Christ, though it is too great to understand fully. Then*
> *you will be made complete with all the fullness of life*
> *and power that comes from God.*
>
> Ephesians 3:18-19 (NLT)

One of the first things I did when I began changing my mindset was learning how to soften my heart. To be clear, this is not something you can do without God. Softening your heart requires you to cry out to the Father and ask Him to change your heart, asking Him to make your heart to be more like Christ.

My childhood was very much a war zone. I never knew when my life was going to be threatened, causing me to run for cover. I didn't know love—true love—freeing love—unconditional love—the Father's love. As a kid, I didn't experience that kind of love. When a healthy person was trying to give me unconditional love, I would sabotage it, push them away, and run as fast as I could. I think I did this because it gave me a false sense of control, but mostly love made me very uncomfortable. The first thing I did besides open myself up to God was I became grateful, which in turn helped me to stay open and accepting. God wants a grateful heart. *How can you start being more grateful?*

Lastly, watch the words you speak over others and yourself. Make sure you are not shaming yourself with such hurtful and hateful words. Break the agreement with shame. Ask yourself those questions and make shame the perpetrator. We talk more about self-compassion, empathy, self-forgiveness, and self-talk in the following chapters, which will help you break or at least distance yourself from shame and guilt.

Prayer: Father God, help me to discern when I am participating with shame and guilt quickly. I do not want to agree with anything other than Your word. Help me to see that I am victorious through You. Father, help me to be more welcoming to all things that come from You. I want to show the world Your light. Please use me to glorify You. In Jesus' name, amen!

CHAPTER 7

Love Your Self

Jesus said to him, "You shall love the Lord your God with all your heart, with all your soul, and with all your mind." This is the first and great commandment. And the second is like it: "You shall love your neighbor as yourself."
Matthew 22:37-39 (NKJV)

Introduction to Loving Yourself!

The Father wants you to love yourself because when you love yourself as the Father loves you, it is easier and possible to love others unconditionally. In the spirit of transparency, I hope the following chapters help you choose to remain loving, kind, compassionate, mindful, forgiving and accepting of yourself and others. I hope you begin to see the importance of speaking life to yourself and others. I hope you learn tactical ways that you will quickly implement, allowing you to change your self-talk, renew your mind to what the Word of God says.

Love

Paul tells us how to showcase love in 1 Corinthians 13:4-8:

Love is patient and kind. Love is not jealous or boastful or proud or rude. It does not demand its own way. It is not irritable, and it keeps no record of being wronged. It does not rejoice about injustice but rejoices whenever the truth wins out. Love never gives up, never loses faith, is always hopeful, and endures through every circumstance. Prophecy and speaking in unknown languages and special knowledge will become useless. But love will last forever!

1 Corinthians 13:4-8 (NLT)

These verses tell us that love is not a feeling but a choice! If you think that you can fall out of love, well, now you know that is a lie from the devil. These verses above teach us how to exemplify love to others and ourselves. Remember, we are to love our neighbors as we love ourselves (Matthew 22:39). Yet, many people are putting a façade on when they interact with their neighbors—meaning they put on a front. Others may be treating their neighbors better than you are treating yourself, and some of you may not be treating your neighbors well at all. Understand that the word "neighbor" here is not only referring to the people you live in proximity to but all the people you meet. If you treat your neighbors with a façade or poorly, then that does provide tremendous insight into how you are also treating yourself. You can only treat others as well as you treat yourself! Some of you are lying to yourself. Saying, "I treat everyone much better than myself." No, you only think you treat people better than yourself. If we were to examine the two, you would probably start seeing many commonalities. Sure, you may be more motivated to behave better when people are looking, so you have to look at the heart attitude, not necessarily the actions. I can say I treat people kindly, but I am judging them and tearing them down in my head. Plus, it is easy to treat a new person or someone you don't often see with kindness for a short period. But it's another thing to show unconditional love to those you are the closest to.

While most believers are familiar with 1 Corinthians 13:4-8, I wonder how do we apply that kind of love to life? We are going to look at exactly how to do that!

Love Yourself Because God Loves You!

In psychology, we would call loving yourself self-love. However, I have already warned you about the dangers of the kingdom of self. Self-love refers to the love, acceptance, and interest of oneself. Now, while that definition is not evil or demonic, the threat comes to play with how it is applied. Here is how sneaky the enemy can be. While God and the devil want you to love yourself, the application and focus are very different. I encourage you to say this quick prayer before we go any further.

Holy Spirit,

As I learn how to love myself as the Godhead desires me to, I ask that you protect me from the spirits who wish me to love myself ungodly. Holy Spirit, help me to see and discern true love. Teach me how to accept and give love to myself and others freely. I ask that You open my eyes of understanding and show me where I may be participating with any ungodly type of love.

In Jesus' name, amen.

There are evil spirits behind lust, whereas there are only right spirits behind true love. Remember, God is love (1 John 4:7:8). Sometimes we may think we are in love or even love something when we are lusting. The easiest way to see the difference is lust takes away, destroys, and involves only the flesh. Whereas love never takes but wants to give.

Additionally, love driven by evil spirits will encourage you to be the god of your own life. In contrast, godly self-love wants you to love and see yourself as the Father sees you. It is about believing, accepting, and owning what God says about you, not what you say about yourself.

Beloved, let us love one another, for love is of God; and everyone who loves is born of God and knows God. He who does not love does not know God, for God is love.

1 John 4:7-8 (NKJV)

You cannot fully love yourself without God. Some people believe they can, and they never arrive. The Unloving Spirit inside of them always remains because only the Father's supernatural love can break it. Those who believe you just need more self-confidence and self-esteem to love yourself entirely are always disappointed. They continue seeking how to be their own god, affirming themselves. They always find that their love is never enough and that they just need to keep gaining more and more self-confidence and self-esteem. Yet, they quickly realize, whether they want to admit it or not, that there is not enough self-confidence or self-esteem to fulfill them. They hunger for more but do not know what it is. Well, it's Jesus!

As human beings, we are going to have hard days and fall short. Jesus promised us hardship on this earth. You may have days where you fall into bondage because of what someone said about you, how your day is going, or due to the reality of life. On those days where you do not like yourself, how are you going to pull yourself out from that? Unless you are in a relationship with Christ, you cannot! You need something bigger than you to pull you out. Jesus provides us with amazing accountability! You need Jesus. On those days, where you feel the world is against you, demonic self-love will not work—only Jesus' love will satisfy you and save you!

The wrong type of self-love will make you self-obsessed. When you are self-obsessed, where is your focus? Your focus is on you, which means it is not on God. Anything that takes you away from Jesus is not of the Father. Please understand, the self-love I am referring to is having a humble perspective of yourself, where you look to the Father to affirm you, not to your own skills, abilities, or talents.

Look at 1 Corinthians 13:4-8. Here Paul is also telling us that the Father wants us to show kindness, compassion, mindfulness, forgiveness, and acceptance towards ourselves. To make this very clear, I will break the verses down over the next few chapters to help you love yourself in a godly way instead of self-righteously.

Love is patient and kind [kindness]. *Love is not jealous or boastful or proud or rude* [compassion and mindfulness]. *It does not demand its own way. It is not irritable, and it keeps no record of being wronged* [forgiveness]. *It does not rejoice about injustice but rejoices whenever the truth wins out. Love never gives up* [acceptance], *never loses faith, is always hopeful, and endures through every circumstance. Prophecy*

and speaking in unknown languages and special knowledge
will become useless. But love will last forever!
1 Corinthians 13:4-8 (NLT)
(brackets added for clarity)

It can take time to pivot from self-hatred to godly self-love, but when you do things God's way—time becomes irrelevant. Even though we humans have to respond to Newton's time, God does not. One of the first things you must do to start seeing yourself as God sees you is to pray to Him often. A staple request in your prayers requires asking Him to change your heart so you can see yourself how He sees you. It takes time to renew your mind. God and the world have a different definition of time. Do not give up. Jesus tells us how important it is for us to continue to pursue a relationship with the Father. He even tells us to keep asking, knocking, and seeking. There may be tough days, but please keep asking the Father to help you see yourself as He sees you.

Ask, and it will be given to you; seek, and you will find; knock,
and it will be opened to you. For everyone who
asks receives, and he who seeks finds, and to him who
knocks it will be opened.
Matthew 7:7-8 (NKJV)

Thinking Traps

Another thing that will be important for you to pay attention to are the thinking traps you fall into. Before discussing the five components in the verses from 1 Corinthians 13:4-8, let's review the thinking traps that may cause you to fall off the righteous path.

Thinking traps are biased perspectives we take on ourselves and the world around us. These thoughts are usually highly irrational and are saturated in the Spirit of Fear. The bottom line is thinking traps are incorrect thinking patterns or believing where you take your eyes off Jesus and on to you or what you do not want to experience. Since you are working to develop a healthy relationship with your inner self, allowing you to stay in the spirit more, it will be quite helpful to identify the faulty thought patterns you most struggle with.

There are about thirteen common thinking traps. I encourage you to highlight or make a note of the ones that most resonate with you. Additionally, as we talk about mindfulness in the next chapter, it will become easier to identify these thinking patterns.

Thirteen Common Thinking Traps:
1. *All-or-Nothing Thinking:* This kind of thinking is more familiar to the perfectionist. It only allows the person to see extremes and no middle ground.

2. *Overgeneralization:* This type of thinking is more subtle as it causes a person to generalize an overall pattern or theme. Sometimes that overgeneralization statement links right back to the all-or-nothing thinking.

3. *Probability Overestimation:* This thinking causes a person to assume something negative will happen, even though they have no proof.

4. *Taking Thoughts as What They Say They Are:* This thinking causes a person to boil down all the history and information to one negative piece of information. They disregard all the years and proof of positive evidence and hyperfocus on one negative thing.

5. *Disqualifying the positives:* This thinking encourages the person to reject the positive experience instead of embracing it. The danger here is when you dismiss the positives. You are encouraging negative thinking patterns only.

6. *Fortune Telling or Mind Reading:* Ultimately, you jump to conclusions without any evidence. You constantly go to the worst-case scenario about anything.

7. *Catastrophizing:* This type of thinking forces a person to overestimate the consequences of something negative happening. Catastrophizing is most prominent among those who struggle with anxiety.

8. *Emotional Reasoning:* You base all your reactions solely on your emotions. It causes the person to take their emotions as facts. *News flash, your emotions can lie to you!*

9. *Should Statements:* This thinking place rigid rules upon you for how you *should* be. It's the belief that you must do something or else you are not good enough. Perfectionists also struggle with this kind of thinking.

10. *Personalization:* This type of thinking causes you to personalize everything you hear, making it about yourself, even when it is not. It is also where you overestimate your influence on an event.

11. *Control Fallacies:* This thinking happens in two ways. First, it is the belief that you have no control over your life and are only a helpless victim. The other is the belief you have *complete* control over your life. Both are false.

12. *"It's Not Fair":* While most people desire a fair world, the reality is there is no standard definition of what fair is. It's failing to accept suffering.

13. *If Only:* This style of thinking causes a person to overfocus on an imagined outcome. It's very linear thinking. If I get this, then I will feel better about myself or my life.

I believe and talk about how thinking traps come from the devil on my podcast. You have to remember humans are not the enemy. If you are not batting against flesh and blood but evil spirits, then that means you are also not battling against yourself, but the evil spirits inside of you.

Next, I want to help you learn how to treat yourself with kindness, compassion, mindfulness, forgiveness, and acceptance. It is easier to identify when the evil spirits are taking hold of you when you can treat yourself with more love. There are days when you will even battle your fleshly desires resulting from the fallen world. I believe it is easier to walk out of this bondage when you do so in the spirit of love, not Fear. Part of responding with godly self-love is learning to rely on the supernatural power of Jesus, walking in Jesus' authority, and how to show yourself the same love He shows you. I do firmly believe when you can love yourself—when you pour into yourself—you can love more and give more to others. Understand pouring into yourself is learning how to do life Jesus' way. Pouring into yourself means learning how to respond and not react. It's learning how to love yourself and operate from a place of love, not fear. It takes time to learn, study, and apply a relationship with Christ in your life.

Father God, thank You for always giving me unconditional love. I want to love as You love. Please help me show Your love to myself and others. I want to shine Your light and love wherever I go. Please give me a revelation on how I can love and accept myself as You do. Please help me be more patient and mindful of myself when I want to reject myself. Most importantly, God, please help me discern when I listen to the evil spirits and not to You!

CHAPTER 8

Self-Kindness

Part of expressing godly love is expressing kindness. Think of the kindest person you know. What attributes do they have that qualify them as being the kindest person you know?

Kindness is expressing generosity, free from expectations. It's showing consideration, support, and being a good friend.

How would you rate your friendship with yourself? Are you best friends, friends, neutral, or enemies? Your answer will give you some great insight into how kind you are towards yourself. Does the idea of hanging out with yourself excite you, or do you notice dread come about you?

Liking yourself is very necessary. It is essential to be a good friend to yourself too! You will be with yourself for the rest of your life, so you better start learning how to like yourself. You must identify all the parts where you are unkind towards yourself and surrender them to God. You must choose to let go of some of the ideals you are chasing and get more in alignment with how God has created you and His will for your life.

Self-kindness is exercising warmth and understanding towards yourself when you suffer, fail, or feel inadequate rather than ignoring your pain or verbally beating yourself with self-criticism.[11] It refers to the tendency to be caring and understanding with yourself rather than harsh and critical. Instead of attacking and berating yourself for your shortcomings, you offer yourself love, warmth, and unconditional acceptance—even when your behavior is unproductive and needs changing.

"Your kindness will reward you, but your
cruelty will destroy you"
(Proverbs 11:17, NLT).

Expressing self-kindness entails treating yourself with understanding and forgiveness. The reality is *no* one is perfect! We all fall short. Instead of getting upset and angry with yourself and others when your expectations are not met, choose to find contentment. The Father asks us to be content in all things. Yes, some days, that is extremely hard. Some days the last thing your flesh wants to do is be kind to another human, and on those days, cry out to Father. Sometimes these days require you to put yourself in time out. Some days I have

---

11 Brown, 2012, p. 131-132.

to put myself in time out until I can rise above my flesh and get back into my spirit. Our flesh is naturally sinful, and on days where I am having a hard time walking in my spirit, I will keep myself in time out communicating with God until I can rise above my flesh! Doing such requires spiritual maturity and discipline, but it's not worth ruining another person's day all because you are having a hard day! Jesus wouldn't want that!

Believing you are perfect and will never fail, nor will others, will only create or increase stress, frustration, criticism, and self-judgment. The bottom line is you are not perfect, and neither are others; so, please get over yourself!

Also, the Bible makes it quite clear we are not to repay evil with evil. Believers are called to live differently than others because we do have help from God.

Don't repay evil for evil. Don't retaliate with insults when people insult you. Instead, pay them back with a blessing. That is what God has called you to do, and he will grant you his blessing.
1 Peter 3:9 (NLT)

Learning how to bless others while expressing kindness and self-control when someone has hurt you requires you to live for Jesus and not for yourself. While you practice living up to 1 Peter 3:9 with the support of the Holy Spirit, also practice showing yourself that command too. The more you practice behaving this way, the easier it will become.

Self-kindness focuses on responding with support and compassion towards yourself when noticing your shortcomings, opposed to responding with criticism. Think of self-kindness as a way to make an internal peace offering that is fueled with warmth, gentleness, and mercy to yourself so that the healing power of the Holy Spirit can take over inside of you.

Common Humanity

There is something known as "shared humanity," which recognizes suffering and feeling personally inadequate is a shared human experience—something we all go through.[12] Even Jesus tells us that we will suffer while on this earth, which is why He left us His peace.

"I am leaving you with a gift—peace of mind and heart. And the peace I give is a gift the world cannot give. So don't be troubled or afraid" (John 14:27, NLT).

We all suffer, and no one enjoys it. Since we all suffer, wouldn't it be best to treat all, even ourselves, with kindness? In a future chapter, I will discuss trials and

---

12 Brown, 2012, p. 132.

tribulations and ways to maintain a perspective of hope during suffering and intense storms.

For years, when I was deep in my victim mindset, it would bother me when I would hear, "you aren't the only one," but now I know that statement is a statement of hope and encouragement. See now when I hear that, I think, "If someone else can overcome it, then so can I." But, before I heard, "Suck it up, there's nothing special about you." Yet, I kept having this subtle thought of where I wanted to be the only one going through what I was going through. Now I was young, maybe eight or nine, and did not have the mental maturity, but now I have tremendous comfort knowing I am not alone. First off, Jesus is always with me. Secondly, even Paul wrote that the temptation you face in your life is no different than another (1 Corinthians 10:13).

Additionally, I leverage the truth that if someone else is dealing with what I am dealing with, then most likely there is also someone out there who has overcome it too with God's help. Somehow this thinking activates me into the Warrior for Christ mentality because it tells me, "If they can do it, then so can I, assuming it's God's will for my life." I become encouraged by it. Even on the off chance, no one has overcome it with God's help. I choose to volunteer to help alleviate others' suffering by empowering them to know they can do all things through Christ. I am passionate about assisting people in seeing how rewarding it is to live for God. I have a deep hunger to be used by God and only to live His will, which is why I only want to glorify Him!

Of course, with spiritual maturity, you learn what God created you to do and what you need to outsource. You learn where you are forcing your will on God and where you are making your own suffering.

Another interesting part about common humanity is everyone feels inadequate. I believe this statement refers to all the humans out there who choose to live self-righteously instead of righteously. I once felt very inadequate about myself, but the more I walk with Christ and see myself as God sees me, the more adequate I see myself.

As mentioned earlier, it is easy for the victim mindset to compare themselves to others. Such thought process comes out of the Unloving Spirit inside of them. They become highly competitive instead of celebrating them. Here is the thing. If another believer "wins," you win too! You have to choose to take a kinder, supportive, and encouraging role. Remember, we live for Him, not for ourselves.

The reality is most people do not like confrontation. Especially because most people also struggle with Fear of man and Fear of rejection. Most people want to be sheep, living their lives not causing any problems.

When that Unloving Spirit kicks into high gear in your mind saying, they are better than you, remember you are both the apple of God's eyes. Instead of feeding into that Unloving Spirit, cheer them on! Remember, they probably feel inadequate about themselves to some degree too. As followers of Christ, we seek to keep peace, bless those that hurt us, and emulate Christ in all we do. Therefore, the better thing you can do is speak life and love over them.

I cannot emphasize enough how much God can help you transform some of your inadequacies. No, you will not ever be perfect, but He can transform and renew your minds in ways you can't even think of! It's so incredible. The reality is we all fail, make mistakes, and participate in some level of dysfunctional behavior; we all are a work in progress.

"Therefore, whatever you want men to do to you, do also to them, for this is the Law and the Prophets"
(Matthew 7:12, NKJV).

Interconnectedness is also another part of common humanity. We are all connected. Paul mentions this in the Bible, too, "The human body has many parts, but the many parts make up one whole body. So it is with the body of Christ" (1 Corinthians 12:12, NLT). "All of you together are Christ's body, and each of you is a part of it" (1 Corinthians 12:27, NLT).

Our suffering and how we handle or do not handle it affects others. So let me take a moment to congratulate you and applaud you for taking responsibility for your suffering and doing something about it by learning how to think like a victor in Christ thinks. If you don't believe this concept, let me challenge your thinking in two ways.

First off, have you ever been highly unkind towards yourself and then went out into the world? Most likely, you were a bit short to people, especially in comparison to those days where you are walking in the Spirit, praising Jesus and blessing everyone that crosses your path. It's just like Proverbs says kindness is rewarding, and cruelty is destructive. On days where you are crueler towards yourself, you are more likely to be harder on other people too. Your words have a higher chance of being used by the enemy to keep someone in bondage. You are impacting society.

Second off, have you ever been in traffic? Of course, you have, and if you haven't, please let me know where you live. It only takes one person to make a poor choice which then impacts the rest of the drivers on the road. No, I'm not saying all accidents or traffic incidents result from this, but some do. In some situations, the choices of others will greatly impact you.

In everything you do, do your best to be kind. In the moments where you can't, call out for God to help you rely on His grace.

And He said to me, "My grace is sufficient for you, for My strength is made perfect in weakness." Therefore most gladly I will rather boast in my infirmities, that the power of Christ may rest upon me.
2 Corinthians 12:9 (NKJV)

Prayer: Father God, help me to exhibit kindness wherever I go. I ask You to examine my heart and identify all the places that need changing. Test me. Use me. Grow me into the person. You want me to be. I want to show kindness and reflect Your light in all situations. Please help me to do this. In Jesus' name, amen.

CHAPTER 9

Self-Compassion

What Is Self-Compassion

Compassion means expressing concern, sensitivity, and care to those enduring suffering accompanied by a deep desire to alleviate their pain. You might not be able to relieve their pain, but you desperately wish you could! It is noticing the suffering of others and freely giving them unconditional love.

Who does this sound like?

> *"The Lord is merciful and gracious,*
> *Slow to anger and abounding in compassion and*
> *lovingkindness"*
> (Psalm 103:8, AMP).

The Godhead: The Father, the Son, and the Holy Spirit! The Father always meets us with compassion, mercy, unconditional love, forgiveness, and so much more. He sees you as the apple of His eye (Psalm 17:8). Do you know what that means—being the apple of God's eye?

Perhaps this picture might help.

I have a Shih-poo named, Moo-Moo and I see him as the apple of my eye, but it's nothing compared to how the Heavenly Father sees His children. My Moo-Moo is so cute and sweet. He loves to cuddle, play, and talk. Oh, and lately, he has grown fond of losing his toys when I am seeing clients. And, you know what? I think he is adorable! Hanging out with this little guy is one of my favorite things to do. Sometimes I can be a bit too obsessed with him. I love him so much. I can't even describe it, but when I try, tears enter my eyes. Guess what! When he messes up or does something he knows not to do, I still see him as the apple of my eye. I still love him. I still think he's awesome! The Father believes all the same and more about you but at an even mightier level. His love is perfect. My love is very far from being perfect. If I imperfectly love my Moo-Moo to this degree, imagine how much more His perfect love feels?

Godly compassion is learning how to see yourself as He sees you! In Luke 6:36 (NLT), Jesus tells us, "You must be compassionate, just as your Father is compassionate." Giving compassion is necessary, and you must give it to yourself as well. It's also learning how to talk to yourself the way He would speak to you. It's learning how to forgive yourself as quickly as He forgives you. It is doing *everything* that God would do to you, to yourself.

Jesus perfectly expressed compassion here on earth too. Mark 5:41-42 depicts the compassion of Jesus:

Taking the child's hand, He said [tenderly] to her, "Talitha kum!"—which translated [from Aramaic] means, "Little girl, I say to you, get up!" The little girl immediately got up and began to walk, for she was twelve years old. And immediately they [who witnessed the child's resurrection] were overcome with great wonder and utter amazement.

Mark 5:41-42 (AMP)

To paint the backstory, Jairus, the local synagogue leader in Capernaum, frantically ran up to Jesus, begging Him to heal his daughter. Jesus followed and spoke those words, and instantly she was resurrected.

Back then, it was considered to be unclean to touch a dead person. The simple act of Jesus touching the dead girl encompasses compassion on its own. Jesus was more concerned with relationships than upholding the letter of the law.

Notice Jesus' power!

What motivated Jesus to use His power over evil spirits, nature, and death? Compassion did! The times when He delivered demon-possessed individuals, spoke to a Samaritan, healed the sick, and raised the dead—all came from a place of compassion!

The Holy Spirit is our advocate. Advocates are change agents. They want to alleviate pain and suffering. The Holy Spirit empowers and encourages you to live like Christ. It is He who changes your heart and helps you to seek the righteous and faithful lifestyle.

Self-compassion is applying compassion to yourself in a godly manner. From just reading about compassion from a godly point of view, what are some ways you can start to show more compassion towards yourself?

Compassion vs. Empathy

Compassion sounds like empathy but is different. The main desire coming from compassion is wanting to alleviate the suffering. Empathy is the ability to relate to another person's pain as if was your own! It's seeing the suffering from another person's shoes and understanding it as they understand it, which can take being overly curious through asking questions to understand how they see it. Some people are naturally born with more compassion and empathy than others. If you cannot begin to comprehend the pain going on in another person's life as if the pain were your own, you might not have a strong sense of empathy. That is okay. Don't beat yourself. Instead, ask for the Father's help. He wants you to be empathetic and compassionate because that is what He gives us. While I know the Holy Spirit will change your heart, you can also practice more mindfulness when you are in emotionally delicate situations.

Ultimately, as believers, we need to express mercy wherever we go, which also means towards ourselves.

Practicing Self-Compassion

Do you know what the opposite of compassion is? Heartlessness! God is not heartless. Therefore, neither should you be heartless towards others or yourself. When you find yourself partaking in belittling, cruel, hateful thoughts, stop it in Jesus' name!

"You can ask for anything in my name, and I will do it so that the Son can bring glory to the Father"
(John 14:13, NLT).

Jesus was motivated by compassion. He got activated and made the changes to alleviate suffering. Part of showing self-compassion towards yourself is doing the work. Is making the necessary changes with the help of the Holy Spirit to show mercy, grace, and forgiveness upon yourself. You have to choose to take steps forwards to obtain the flourishing well-being and life the Father desires for you.

Here are some things you can do to start growing your ability to showcase others and your compassion.

The more compassionate you are to yourself, the more compassionate you will be to someone else.

1. Start consciously checking in more with your thoughts. Start asking yourself: Would I say what I am thinking to a friend? Would I treat a friend the way I am treating myself?

2. Get proactive. Identify where you are currently suffering and identify what is in your control to alleviate it. Suffering is a part of life, but we can bring additional and unnecessary suffering to our life too. But please note there may be times where you will have to experience suffering that only God can alleviate. However, there are still some things you can do. Like, find ways to be kinder towards yourself. You can learn how to trust the Father more in that discomfort or pain you are experiencing. Being proactive about alleviating your suffering will not always look like a tangible external action but an internal choice or focus.

3. Keep a journal. Start to identify the triggers in your life that causes you to agree with those evil spirits.

4. Reframe your inner dialogue. Since most people do not want to train or prepare before the gremlins attack, I encourage you to do this now. When the self-hatred thoughts come because you over-

ate or whatnot, what are you going to say to yourself? Go ahead and write out that script. Or better yet, go and identify a scripture you will say when the attacks come.

For years I battled self-hatred when I ate, let alone overate. It's not too surprising seeing I signed a contract with the devil to have an eating disorder. Finally, I decided that what the enemy was trying to get me to desire and chase after was unattainable. I broke the agreement with the devil and then worked to renew my mind. When those thoughts came causing me to hate and reject myself, I would say to them, *No! I might not look like I want yet, but I am working on getting there. Jesus loves me. Jesus, I give You this, do what you want with it and make my heart agree with Your will.* In time and with the Father's help, I learned how to walk out of such hate talk. I had to want to let go of my will, though, too. For a long time, I only wanted what I wanted. I didn't want to let go of my ideal body, but then I decided to give all of me all my dreams, desires, ideals—to Him!

5. Cry out to the Father. Pray and don't stop! There will be days where the best thing for you to do is curl up on Jesus' lap. He knows what you are going through, and He wants to help you to victory.

Part of compassion is refraining from judging yourself and others. Jesus showed us how powerful it is to take a more objective, forgiving, and honest perspective. We see this when He asked the crowd the following:

"They kept demanding an answer, so he stood up again and said, 'All right, but let the one who has never sinned throw the first stone!'"
(John 8:7, NLT)

Remember, it is God's place to judge. That means you can stop judging yourself. Tell those evil spirits to go in Jesus' name. Find a plan to help defeat these spirits with the help of Jesus Christ and implement it as you walk it out and experiment with the best method of attack. Never refrain from showing compassion. When you exercise compassion, you're helping to portray God's love!

Prayer: Father God, help me to show myself and others the compassion You showed me. Help me to love myself as You love me. Please help me to see myself and others as You see them. Father, I ask that You help me identify when I am heartless towards myself and others. Please change my heart to Your will. Remove anything that is not of You and help me to discern them as well.

CHAPTER 10

Mindfulness

"Set your minds on things that are above,
not on things that are on earth"
(Colossians 3:2, ESV).

We only exist right here, right now. You may be thinking of things you have to do later today, things you are excited about, or even dreading doing. Or maybe you are thinking about your past and how you wished you responded. Whatever you are thinking about, know you only exist right here, right now—this very moment is the present moment you are occupying. As much as we can guess a calculated prediction, we do not know if we will be alive or dead in the next three hours to thirty years. Therefore, the best thing we can do is learn how to stay present on today.

And who of you by worrying can add one hour to [the length of] his life? And why are you worried about clothes? See how the lilies and wildflowers of the field grow; they do not labor nor do they spin [wool to make clothing],
Matthew 6:27-28 (AMP)

Personal history significantly impacts people's behavioral responses. However, that is until you decide to see your emotional baggage as a hindrance, not a protector. Once you arrive at this place, it is easier to renew your mind because you are hungry to live a more excellent way.

For example, maybe you beat yourself up when you make mistakes. Or perhaps you are someone who struggles with anger, so your inner voice criticizes you when you blow up over something equivalent to spilled milk. Or maybe you find yourself judging others and personalizing other people's choices. Whatever the thinking trap is, you must start to investigate it mindfully. Ask yourself:

What triggers me to behave this way? What do I not like about it? What keeps me continuing with such behavior? What can I do instead?

Invite the Holy Spirit in and ask the Spirit to help you understand what is behind some of your behaviors.

Now, before you go blaming your genes, know this. While science has said, our behaviors are partly due to genetics. Know that you can change them too. Very little of you is hardwired, and this makes sense because if you were hardwired, how could you ever renew your mind or operate in the mind of Christ? How could you ever emulate Christ if God designed humans to be hardwired?

Your genetic makeup can change based on minute-to-minute thinking and choices. Dr. Caroline Leaf, a cognitive neuroscientist specializing in neuropsychology, has scientifically proven that genes may create an environment within us, but genes do not produce the problem. We produce the problem through our choices. It's our choices that figuratively unzip our DNA, which is why you may be prone to act that way. Genes do not control you.[13] Just like your emotions do not control you. You control your genes, and you control your emotions. Perhaps this is why there is a theme in the Bible that articulates we can control our thoughts too!

Dr. Leaf (2013), in her book *Switch on Your Brain*, explains the true phenomenon of genes by stating that genes are constantly being remodeled based on your response to life experiences. You hold the power!

Your thoughts, imagination, and choices can change the structure of your brain on every level. I'm talking

---

13 Leaf, 2013.

molecular, genetic, epigenetic, cellular, structural, neurochemical, electromagnetic, and even subatomic. Essentially you are designed to do your own brain surgery.[14] Perhaps, this is also why self-awareness, mindfulness, self-compassion, self-acceptance, and self-forgiveness are critical. When you are aware of your thoughts and respond lovingly towards yourself, you can make the necessary life changes you crave.

What Is Mindfulness and How to Apply It

Mindfulness is intentionally paying attention to the present moment, free from judgment. It's observing others and your own thoughts, feelings, sensations, and emotions with curiosity, free from judgment, closed, or bias thinking. Mindfulness and acceptance coexist because you have to be willing to be open to whatever sensations or thoughts come up. Ultimately, the theme of mindfulness is to develop a nonjudgmental persona!

Therefore you have no excuse or justification, everyone of you who [hypocritically] judges and condemns others; for in passing judgment on another person, you condemn yourself, because you who judge [from a position of arrogance or self-righteousness] are habitually practicing the very same things [which you denounce].
Romans 2:1 (AMP)

---

14 Leaf, 2013.

Additionally, practicing mindfulness helps to create and strengthen your conscious awareness. Conscious awareness is deliberately focusing your attention on what is happening right here, right now. Essentially you are observing and refraining from judging, either yourself or others. What's judging? Judging is when you make inaccurate and unfair assessments of people without adequate information, which usually leads us to decide if we like the person based on what they did or didn't do. It is human nature to judge others for exactly what we do, which is why Jesus calls this hypocritical.

Observation is simply observing how someone is acting and not providing conclusions on why they act that way. When you add observing to mindfulness, I have found your emotional state naturally balances. There are one thousand plus reasons why someone may have just cut you off in traffic. Before you go down the path of judgment saturated with the victim mindset, choose to go down mindfully observing. It is here where you can come up with a handful of possibilities because that is all they will ever be—a possibility. For instance, maybe the driver didn't mean to, or perhaps they were rushing to an emergency. Or maybe they are having a bad day and are currently fighting the Spirit of Fear. Whatever it is, pray for them wishing them peace and safety.

Mindfulness is a powerful intervention that can help you decrease many by-products of the Spirit of Fear.

Practicing mindfulness can help with stress management, depression, anxiety, overcoming trauma, and aids in emotional intelligence and resilience. Mindfulness can also help you preserve bandwidth, allowing you to be more productive. When you can learn how to be present and free from stress or worry, it's incredible how much more bandwidth you gain.

Practicing mindfulness will not hinder but enhance your well-being. Now take note that I said the word practice. You have to *consciously* practice the new behaviors for you to transform yourself into a victor. Mindfulness is working to find a harmonious approach to make sure your negative feelings and thoughts are not suppressed, exaggerated, or handled critically but observed and acknowledged. Many times, our feelings and emotions are very similar to a two-year-old having a tantrum. In fact, your amygdala, which is your emotion storehouse, is located in the limbic system of your brain, and scientists have said it has the emotional maturity of a two or three-year-old.[15]

When we have an emotional response and work to avoid it, suppress it, or ignore it, guess what happens? The emotional sensation usually almost always becomes more intense and more robust. Therapists often refer to this as a gremlin because he maintains his cuteness and kindness until you pour water on this guy. Still, once

15 Hopper, 2018.

he gets wet—you ignore or suppress him—he then becomes a mean, nasty, ugly, and terrifying gremlin. The same can be said when two-year-olds have tantrums. Am I right? Man, they can be the cutest thing ever, but if you ignore them or do not nurture and acknowledge them when they have an emotional response, they will freak out! Your mature brain is not very different.

However, as believers, you know what this gremlin is indeed referring to? Spiritual warfare!

What do you do when your gremlin is trying to highjack your mind? Remember, avoidance only increases our suffering. Plus, where did Jesus practice avoidance? Here is a list of a few things you can do to create distance from that gremlin and get back in control of yourself. These techniques all include mindfulness at some layer.

1. Pray. Surrender to God. Ask for His help. Usually, when things are really bad with the gremlin, we do not want to pray, but it's the best thing. Just like a cranky two-year-old fights a nap! The reality is you need the Father's help to get a grip! Sometimes the spirals come on so hard that the only thing that will break it and bring you back is the Father's love.

---

*"Therefore submit to God. Resist the devil
and he will flee from you"*
(James 4:7, NKJV).

Notice James says, *first* submit to God, which occurs when we pray. And, then he will flee. God's power is no joke!

2. Find a verse that helps you combat whatever you are feeling. For instance, if you are anxious or worried, try one of these:

I let the peace of God into my heart, and I refuse to worry about anything. Instead, I am grateful for all (Colossians 3:15).

I refuse to let my heart be troubled. Instead, I cast all my problems on to Him because my Father unconditionally loves me and wants to help me in every area (John 14:1; 1 Peter 5:7).

Using scripture will always get you better results.

3. Talk back to the gremlin! Let's use an example for this one. Imagine you are about to give a speech in front of twenty people or two hundred people. You notice the anxiety is rising as your turn to speak draws closer. Instead of ignoring the anxiety and telling yourself you aren't anxious, mindfully focusing on saying this:

"Hey, little anxiety dude (I am visualizing this moment and this gremlin, and I even will rub his belly or head). *I see you, and I hear you, but I will give you all the attention as soon as possible, but right now, I am going just to put you right here* (mentally place gremlin to the side). *I have not forgotten about you. I need to focus on my speech because doing this*

is a high value of mine. The second the speech is over, I will talk with you, okay?"

Doing this allows you to acknowledge how you feel without coming into agreement with it. Similar to acknowledging or tending to the two-year-old before the little one goes in a full-blown tantrum. Please note accepting and agreeing are two different things. You can accept a feeling as part of you and not come into agreement with it. For example, if I feel exhausted, I can acknowledge that fatigue, maybe even take a break, but I don't have to act on what it may be telling me, which could be "stop working, and relax." The second I come into agreement with that feeling of exhaustion—exhaustion has won. What can I do instead? Again, mindfully acknowledge that exhaustion and then say I choose to feel productive. Your body might be feeling exhausted, and that's okay, but your spirit is on fire. Remember the same Spirit that raised Christ from the dead dwells in you. To clarify, I am not telling you to ignore your emotions as they do give you insight. At some point, you will need to take a rest. The question becomes, are you being enticed by your flesh or encouraged by your Spirt Man?

The Spirit of God, who raised Jesus from the dead, lives in you. And just as God raised Christ Jesus from the dead, he will give life to your mortal bodies by this

same Spirit living within you.
Romans 8:11 (NLT)

---

4. Leverage your values. When you make choices based on your values, you move toward the person you want to be. If you are not sure how to do this or what they are, do not fret. To figure out your values, run through the following questions below by providing three responses. Keep it simple by noting the first thing that comes to mind. Once you are done, find all the similarities, and those are your current values.

How do you fill your space?
How do you spend your time?
How and where do you spend or exert your energy?
How and where do you spend your money?
Where are you most organized, diligent?
Where are you most reliable?
What dominates your thoughts?
What do you visualize most that has happened?
What do you most often talk to yourself about?
What do you most often talk to others about?
What inspires you?
What goals that you have reached stand out in your life and have stood the test of time?
What do you love to learn, research, study or read about most?

5. Stopping owning your symptoms. Now, let's say you have a headache. You notice the pain coming on, and someone asks, "What's wrong?" The Bible reminds us how powerful and life-provoking words are. God even created this world through releasing words. Jesus healed people by releasing words too. Saying, "I have a headache," articulates ownership and agreement. While it might sound silly, you must put tremendous distance between "I have" or "I am" and the symptom. Instead, say, "My body's head has a headache, but I am healed by Jesus' stripes" (1 Peter 2:24).

Here's the thing, it's easy to fall into legalism with this one. The point is to hold on to Jesus' healing more than your pain or symptoms. When you see yourself as not owning the health matter, it can be easier to remember you are healed. If you do say, "I have a headache," know you are not releasing anything into the air. The truth is this encouragement about not owning your symptoms is more to help you remember to thank Jesus for His healing power. I'm not saying you need to deny your feelings; it's saying you are healed through Him. It is easy to deny Jesus' truth when sickness comes about, which is why you must hold on to the truth: you are healed by His stripes! See yourself as healed, not sick.

When your thoughts and feelings are painful or produce stress, it's normal not to want to maintain a receptive, open, curious, and even playful mental space regarding these private moments. You may try to avoid or eliminate thoughts like that, which increases more suffering. When you avoid your pain or stress-creating thoughts, you are participating in avoidance. I promise avoidance only makes life worse. Practicing avoidance only moves you from a typical experience of despair to one of suffering and ineffective action. Personally, when I sense anxiety knocking on my mental door regarding a task, I have control over; avoiding the tasks only makes my life harder. Ultimately, I grow more anxious. What kills the anxiety is choosing to be proactive. When I outline the steps I need to take to complete the project, I quickly see a way. In turn, the anxiety dissipates. Choosing to be proactive will always foster better fruit.

How do you accept and even embrace these potentially painful private moments? It comes down to fearlessly and courageously facing them! I have this mantra I say in outwardly unpleasant situations, *"This, too, shall pass."* And guess what it always does. Now, as for the private moments, that is when I practice mindfulness and compassion towards myself. I also always pray. If you study the behaviors of Jesus, you will quickly learn He remains in constant prayer and communication with the Father. If Jesus can do it, so can you! You have to start remembering to pray about everything. Prayer is the answer!

Father God, I see how I don't look to You for everything, and I want to change that. I ask you to come into every area of my life. When I don't want to let You in, please remind me that You love me and want to help me. Father, show me how to be mindful and not judgmental in every situation. Please help me to see life as You see it! In Jesus' name, amen.

CHAPTER 11

Self-Forgiveness

What Is Forgiveness

A mentor of mine once said, "Forgiveness means you forever give up the right to bring up another person's as well as your past hurtful actions." Such a point is in the Bible too. When you choose to remind another person of their mistakes, more than likely, you are still in bondage about the ordeal. Now, yes, it is possible to bring something up lovingly and kindly to help another see their mistakes so they can learn from them, assuming you are mature and wise enough to navigate this. Of course, you shouldn't be doing the very thing they are struggling with either. However, it comes down to intention. Sometimes when we bring up stuff from the past that we have said we have forgiven the person for, we hope to hurt them, not help them. Intention and motive matter!

If you are not to the point where you can forever let the pain and past of what you or a person has done, then do not say, "I forgive you." Instead, keep praying to

God for Him to change your heart about the situation. Jesus reminds us how important it is for our words to exhibit our intentions. Now, yes, sometimes we accept an apology, not knowing we haven't healed from the pain. That's okay. We are all growing, which is why we all need to give one another more grace.

When you say you forgive someone, you cancel a debt. Imagine if God kept bringing up your sins?

Here is the thing, God makes it very clear that if you are unwilling to forgive others, He is unwilling to forgive you too!

"But if you do not forgive others their sins,
your Father will not forgive your sins"
(Matthew 6:15, NIV).

It's choosing to turn the other cheek and put your resentment, anger, and desire to retaliate or get revenge away by giving it to God. It's separating the sin from the person. God created humans to be saints before Him. It is through sin that humans have separated themselves from God. He didn't create us to be sinners. Therefore, you need to remember to remove the sins of a person from the person! Again, no one is perfect. We do not fight against flesh and blood but evil spirits. If you can learn to see it was an evil spirit or the flesh that drove the person to behave that way, it can be easier to navigate forgiveness. Yes, that person chose to agree with those spirits, but there is a walking out period for all. Sometimes we don't feel like we chose to agree with the enemy. Before anyone can make a change, they have to see a change needs to be made.

My old self has been crucified with Christ. It is no longer I who live, but Christ lives in me. So I live in this earthly body by trusting in the Son of God, who loved me and gave himself for me.
Galatians 2:20 (NLT)

When you are crucified with Christ, you agree to surrender to Jesus in all aspects of your sinful life! Essentially, you see that they died on the cross with Christ. Next, your focus becomes completely surrendering to living as the Father desires you to. It's ending the self-center lifestyle the world screams and living a Christ-centered life.

Jesus now lives in you through the Holy Spirit. It is He who fills up all the empty places that you turn over to Him. At the same time, the Spirit enters us when we first believe in Jesus. You will constantly have to deny your sinful desires and choose to pick up your cross and carry it! Meaning you will need to go the route that Jesus wants you to go, not the route your flesh desires.

Sometimes it appears we over apologize and forgive, but the reality is we may not be sorry and may not have forgiven yet. Forgiveness is very similar to love. *It's a choice.* A choice free from conditions or ultimatums, and you must use your self-control with it too. We must choose to forgive. Sometimes it is super hard because we have to move through life, taking our thoughts captive on a second-to-second basis. I get it. It can be super exhausting and challenging to do the "living" part of life while fighting the spiritual battles. Again, rely on God's grace, not your own strength.

Let me ask you this. When you mess up or need forgiveness, don't you want to be forgiven and then move on with your life? I know I do. I can't stand when someone throws a past action, especially when I was a different person, in my face. When you sin and wholeheartedly ask for repentance, don't you appreciate that God forgives you without condemnation? Of course, you do. We all want to be forgiven. No one wants to have to argue for it or fight for it.

God wants you to do the same for other people and yourself. Remember, no one is perfect. As humans, we are going to make mistakes. We are going to fail—we are not perfect and never will be. However, forgiveness frees us from condemnation. Luke 7:40-41 reminds us of those who forgive much, love much. And isn't that the point to continuously operate from a place of love?

When you forgive someone, you are not undermining or ignoring the fact they did something wrong. It does not mean what the person did was not wrong. Choosing to forgive does not diminish the other person's wrongdoings. We are not talking about denial amid pain but learning how to let go and move forward. Also, trust that God will redeem the situation!

Do you see how kindness, compassion, mindfulness, and even acceptance work in this too? Choosing to let go and forgive is more for you than for the other person. Bitterness is a dangerous place to be. It contains unforgiveness, resentment, retaliation, anger, hatred, violence, and even murder. Plus, it creates a whole lot of unnecessary stress in your life.

One thing I found to be extremely interesting is how we can now link unforgiveness to health problems. Disease is where you are uneasy, and when you are outside of the easement, your body becomes troubled or uncomfortable, which is what sickness does to your body. Do you know where you are at the most ease? When you are in a relationship with the Father. His umbrella protects you!

Unforgiveness starts to eat away at your soul as cancer cells do in the body. The reality is unforgiveness is a spiritual problem, not a psychological one.

You know you have successfully forgiven another when your feelings turn from heartless to warm, loving, compassionate, and understanding about the situation. This requires help from the Father and choosing to see different perspectives, which can take time. Preferably ones where you do not personalize the situation. And remember, when you accepted Christ, you agreed to do life His way. The question is, are you going to strive to uphold your side?

When you forgive and allow God to give you strength to maintain the forgiveness, you become strong, not weak. Forgiveness takes effort. Whereas not forgiving is the path of the least resistance. Forgiveness is an attitude of the heart, not a performance of the mind.

What Are Some Reasons to Forgive?

Forgiveness frees you! If you don't believe me, think about a time where your heart was unforgiving towards someone. Do you have that moment in your mind? Great, now quickly take a body scan. Notice how you remember your heart having more contention and pain. Perhaps you even recall feeling stressed, upset, angry, and tense with pain in your heart.

As you think about this memory, let me ask you— during this time when that memory was occurring in your present life, how much did you think about the action against you? If you are anything like me, those thoughts of unforgiveness would come, and they would come hard. All I could do was think about what had been done to me, which made me angry and stole many extraordinary present moment opportunities from me. Hmm, doesn't that sound like the devil's plan? The events that hurt me constantly filled my head, and I was hurting. However, when I chose to take those unforgiving thoughts into captivity and forgive my perpetrator, peace slowly came over me. Nowadays, I barely remember my abusive childhood. It is pretty challenging for me to recall all the hardships I endured because I spent more of my time asking the Father to take it from and me and help me forgive!

I pulled up the weeds of unforgiveness and planted seeds of forgiveness which in time grew to be a beautiful crop and allowed me the freedom to move forward in my life. Of course, none of this would have happened if I didn't surrender to doing it Jesus' way!

Now, sometimes you have to replant that seed a few times because it does not land on great soil, but that is okay. Be persistent, and don't give up. Know every time you choose to walk down forgiveness, you are figuratively watering those seeds. The more you choose to walk down the path of life, the more you water those seeds.

When you choose to participate in unforgiveness, you decide to hand that perpetrator the keys to your inner world. They gain power over you, and you become a slave to them mentally. I don't know about you, but

I refuse to hand the power of my life over to anyone but Jesus. God is the only one I want to have power and control over me. I refuse to give that over to someone willingly.

Who do you need to forgive?

Prayer: Father God, if I have any unforgiveness in my heart that I am not aware of, help me to see it, and please take it away from me. I give it to You. Help me quickly to forgive as You do. Please help me to do that. Forgive me for not forgiving others. I see the errors of my ways. Help me to live like You in all areas of my life. Search my heart and soul and help me to see where I am out of alignment with Your will. In Jesus' name, amen.

Applying Forgiveness

Forgiving others and even yourself consists of practicing understanding, mindfulness, acceptance, kindness, empathy, and compassion. But ultimately, forgiving others and yourself is the result of having a deep relationship with Christ. You have to desire to live for Him more than you wish to live for yourself.

I think we are all guilty of doing stuff, and once we become cognitive and in control of ourselves again, we have no idea why we did what we did. Sometimes we as humans do not always think things through. Parents sometimes have to teach kids to think before they speak and do because there is an equal or greater reaction for every action. It takes time to crucify the flesh, and we must learn how to do it! Jesus will show you!

What you do will affect you, and you may not like it. The process of forgiveness is a conceptualized internal process. An individual who has experienced a transgression chooses to let go of the negative feelings associated with the act and the perpetrator. Imagine yourself giving it to Jesus and letting Him deal with the situation. He's a better redeemer and judge than you could ever be.

However, as I briefly mentioned above, forgiveness is a heart attitude, not a mental attitude. Sometimes we may forgive mentally before our heart has been able to forgive. When we say, "I *forgive* you," we must make sure it is because your heart wants to forgive, followed by your mind. When we mentally forgive before forgiving in our hearts, we tend to keep replaying the event on repeat in our heads.

When you are struggling to forgive someone, before impulsively saying you forgive them, try this. First, acknowledge the hurt to the transgressor. Let them know you hear their apology, assuming they are indeed and that they want forgiveness. Let them know you plan to forgive them entirely, but you need time to talk to God and heal. There is nothing wrong with that. It is better you tell someone the truth than say you forgive them when you don't because that can, and usually does, damage the relationship.

So then, how do you get your heart to catch up with your mind? First, pray! God will be far more helpful than anything else. One thing that works for me is putting myself in the other person's shoes; this is practicing empathy. I use mindfulness and compassion to help me get insight into what they were thinking or what drove them. I also have to forgo my prideful thinking of *"what an idiot, I'd never do that"* because, in all honesty, I do not know what I would do if I were in the same situation. It is easy to glamorize that I wouldn't. I can only assume I would not.

I also remember God has forgiven me, and He commands me to forgive others. Such realization propels me to forgive the other. Therefore, when I choose to remain in unforgiveness, I am sinning. The funny thing about forgiveness is the more you can practice forgiving, and the more you can take your thoughts captive, the easier forgiving someone becomes. Forgiveness is like a muscle we have to strengthen. Many people will tell you to forgive, but do not forget. Well, that is not how heart forgiveness—the attitude of forgiveness—works. When you forgive but do not forget, you cannot forgive in your heart because as a man thinks in his heart, so he is. When you dwell on those painful memories, you are reinforcing potential bitterness and anger within yourself. The thoughts of the past will come, but we are to live in the present, not the past. When the ideas come, take them captive. If you cannot do that, at least mindfully notice the thoughts as a moving cloud. Remind yourself you have forgiven that person and move forward with your life.

Dr. Clinton and Dr. Hawkins (2009), professional counselors, encourage you to think of forgiving and letting go like this:

> *Remember to forget.* We will never entirely forget the transgressions against us, but we can decrease the strength of the memory. When someone reminds you of the offenses made against you, respond by saying, *"I distinctly remember forgetting that,"* and then move forward.
> Clinton & Hawkins[16]

Now, if you are thinking, "I hear what you are saying, but what about when a person continues to repeat the same transgression repeatedly. Do I still forgive them?" My answer is yes. There is a difference between forgiving someone allowing that individual to stay in your life and forgiving someone but not allowing that person to remain in your life. To clarify, I am talking about abuse, cruelty, or anything else that puts your life in jeopardy. If your spouse continues to fail to communicate effec-

---

16 Clinton & Hawkins, 2009, p. 128.

tively, then you need to give them grace. Talk to God about it. Ask the Father to change your heart. He might be trying to work out something in you, anyways.

We all need boundaries. If someone is constantly asking for forgiveness and apologizing but is not correcting or working to change their behavior, I would encourage you to put healthy boundaries up to protect yourself. There is nothing wrong with protecting yourself. If someone is physically, sexually, emotionally, and psychologically abusing you, you do need to set boundaries and remove that person from your life. The person cannot come back into your life until they have corrected their ways and allowed time for healing to occur in both of you. If you cannot get out, please search for groups or nonprofits that help women and men get out of abusive situations. You are not alone, there are people who want to help you, but you have to help yourself too!

Now, self-forgiveness is no different than forgiving someone else. It is simply choosing to let go of your mistakes and move forward when you mess up. You acknowledge it and move forward in your life. Sometimes, when I am upset at myself for making a poor choice after learning more information, I remind myself that I made the best decision I could with the variables I had. If I didn't, I learn from it. Experiential learning is the best kind sometimes.

Sometimes remembering the commitment we made to forgive others or ourselves can be challenging, which is why I encourage you to do one of two things:

1. On your phone or in a journal, I want you to create a page that says, "I have forgiven…"

Anytime forgiveness needs to occur, and you have committed to forgiving the transgressor in your heart, I want you to write down their name, why you forgive them, but not what they did. Next to that, write the date of when you forgave them. If those thoughts as to why you should not forgive someone comes up, I want you to read that person's name saying, I *forgive* _____, followed by why you forgive them and on the date you forgave them.

2. *Dr. Clinton & Hawkins (2009) suggest having "Stones of Remembrance" or a concrete item to remind you of your forgiveness.* This comes from the Bible. When God parted the Jordan River allowing the Israelites to travel to dry land, God told Joshua to have each tribe choose a stone to be piled up as a memorial to what great things God had done that day. Those stones served as a remembrance for the people and their children in times to come. For some people having a tangible item makes it easier for them to recall they have forgiven.

Which option is best for you? Both work. Perhaps try both!

Unforgiveness is a behavior. If you are struggling to forgive others, you are probably struggling to forgive yourself too, which only keeps you in bondage. We cannot stop people from hurting us, but we can improve our response to it. Remember, we are to maintain the power God has given us in our life, and when we do not forgive, we forfeit our keys over.

Prayer: Father God, help me to forgive as You forgive. Help me to see people as You see them. I want a heart that quickly forgives and always shows love. Please change my heart to be the heart You want me to have. When I want to be unforgiving, please remind me to forgive because You have forgiven me. Thank You for all You are doing in my life, and I ask You to continue guiding me in every area of my life. In Jesus' name, amen.

CHAPTER 12

Self-Acceptance

We all have thoughts, painful memories, or things we don't like about ourselves, as already discussed. We sometimes work exceptionally hard to avoid them. But, kindness, compassion, mindfulness, forgiveness, and acceptance help you move even further away from avoidance, which only promotes more suffering.

Acceptance means allowing your thoughts, feelings, and circumstances to come as they are without trying to change them to what you prefer. You don't have to like the situation. Your opinion of the matter is frankly irrelevant. Acceptance is more about letting go of control or the desire to want to control the situation. It is learning how to hold yourself in an unconditional positive regard regardless of what is occurring around you.

You will discover when you practice accepting yourself and say what God says about you, even if it is not completely real to you yet, you will become more encouraged to work on yourself. Self-acceptance leads to self-improvement, which means you are choosing to act, hopefully where God is guiding you too.

Choosing to have unconditional positive regard towards yourself—is also expressing unconditional self-love. The Father sees you in a positive light. Did you know when you sin, He forgives you and sees past the sin to see you! He loves the sinner but hates the sin.

Remember, we are to love our neighbor as we love our self. The psychological aspect of acceptance occurs when an individual becomes willing to accept a particular situation as it exists—without judgment.

Self-acceptance is influential when it comes to declaring our self-worth. Usually, our self-worth is lower when we are struggling to accept ourselves because it does not match our ideal self, and therefore we reject ourselves. There will be many days where you may not like your reality, and you can choose to fight it, getting nowhere, or to find contentment and allow the Lord to be your joy and strength. The choice is yours!

There is a slight difference between self-esteem and self-acceptance. I discuss self-esteem in greater detail in the next chapter, but here is a small glimpse. Self-esteem is how someone evaluates and feels about themselves. Questions like *"Am I smart? Am I attractive? Am I good at anything?"* are questions that reflect self-esteem. It's ultimately your opinion of yourself.

The focus of self-acceptance emphasizes that you accept and value who you are with unconditional love as the Father does. This needs to happen regardless of how you act in a moment, achieve a satisfactory standard, or reach your life ideals. It's giving yourself grace and focusing on what you can change!

Due to social media, the pressure of society, and the culture you live in, it can be quite challenging to accept yourself when the world tells you through subliminal messaging you are not good enough or doing life right. First off, remember the devil is the god of this world (2 Corinthians 4:4), which is why you must remember to do what Paul says in Romans 12:2,

---

Don't copy the behavior and customs of this world but let God transform you into a new person by changing the way you think. Then you will learn to know God's will for you, which is good and pleasing and perfect.
Romans 12:2 (NLT)

Paul clearly states that believers are not to respond or behave as the world does. We have a supernatural power at our disposal. Decided to use your free will to keep asking, seeking, and knocking (Matthew 7:7)! Besides, the world is constantly changing. God is not! There are so many conflicting opinions and thoughts out there. It's confusing and hard to maneuver when you listen to everyone or anyone but God. He's the only one who doesn't change. He's the very definition of consistency, and if you dislike change, you should love God because He doesn't change!

While this is not godly, men are very much told from a young age their worth lies in their accomplishments and being the family's breadwinner. Women are shown from a young age as well the significance of their look and size. Do yourself a favor and stop trying to live as the world encourages. You cannot play for both teams. You must decide whose team you will play on and then be a good teammate and practice! I hope you pick God's side. The cool thing about His side is you won't practice alone. He will help you in everything you do if you let Him!

"Do not love the world or the things in the world. If anyone loves the world, the love of the Father is not in him"
(1 John 2:15, NKJV).

Again, basing your self-worth and self-acceptance on the world's standard is very dangerous. Your worth is immeasurable. Jesus died for you! You cannot measure your worth. It's not a variable—it's a constant—it's the truth. Jesus died for you because of how much you mean! To the Father, you are priceless, which is why He sent His Begotten Son. He wanted to rescue you! That's pretty incredible. That's how worthy you are—Jesus suffered for you to have freedom! Are you going to take it?

Take the one thing you love more than anything and imagine it being so severely beaten that it is unrecognizable. Meanwhile, as this beloved thing is being beaten and tortured, you watch and cannot interfere because you know the suffering will bring tremendous victory for many. That is what God allowed to happen to His only Son because of how much you are worth to Him. He loved you that much, and nothing has changed.

You cannot measure your worth because it is not dependent on performance, degrees, financial status, behavior, titles, possessions, or anything else. Solomon talks about how vain it is to find worth and satisfaction in anything other than the Father in Ecclesiastes. The only thing that will create ultimate worth inside of you is a relationship with Christ.

Your worth was created by God and is maintained through God. If you struggle to see your worth the way God sees it—if you give strangers the power to define if you are worthy or not—remember this: An outsider cannot see all the components inside of you that build up the "self." They are only making judgments based on assumptions that can never contain all the facts of who you are. Besides, only the Father knows how many hairs are on your head. If He knows that level of detail about you, isn't it wiser to trust what He says than a mere mortal?

"And the very hairs on your head are all numbered.
So don't be afraid; you are more valuable to God
than a whole flock of sparrows"
(Luke 12:7, NLT).

One part of you does not declare if you are worthy or unworthy. The only thing that knows you better than yourself is your Creator. And, He says you are worthy!

Allow God into every area of your life and start saying what He says. It's the truth anyway! He's the only Spirit that is more of an *expert* on you than you are. He never withholds information from you either.

I appreciate what psychologist Albert Ellis has to say regarding the push and pull dynamic of how self-acceptance impacts self-worth.

"The doctrine of variable worth: Here's what worth is really about: Worth is a philosophical idea, not a yardstick. Worth is based on self-judgment. Worth is a constant, not a variable."[17]

Isn't that the truth? I mean, think back to what God did to His only Son for you!

Life, in many ways, is binary in a few aspects. You are either in the kingdom of light or darkness, speaking life or death, operating in love or fear. The same goes

---

17 Smart Recovery, n.d., para. 10.

for how you view yourself. You are either accepting or rejecting yourself. When you reject yourself, you're going to not only live in fear of people rejecting you, but you may attract people who will reject you as well. I encourage you to start loving yourself by beginning to accept yourself as you are. Please understand choosing to accept yourself does not mean you aren't working to change that bad behavior or thing you don't like about yourself. It's simply acknowledging where you are currently, and doing so can help facilitate the changes you are trying to make. I want you to love yourself as God loves you, and He says you are *incredible!* He thinks you are so freaking awesome. Let me ask you, where can you be more accepting of yourself?

The best way to practice acceptance is by consciously taking different perspectives. What are some other ways you can see whatever it is you are not accepting? Try seeing it the way God sees it. What does God say about it anyway? The more you practice seeing things from new perspectives, the more you increase your ability to practice mental flexibility.

Prayer: Father God, I want to accept myself as you accept me, but I don't know how. Would you please show me how to do this? In moments where I am rejecting myself, please speak to me. Let me see that I am talking badly of Your masterpiece. Thank You for helping me accept myself and unconditionally love myself as you love me. In Jesus' name, amen.

CHAPTER 13

What is Self-Esteem

Self-esteem refers to the experience that you are suitable for life and the requirements of life. It is having an inner sense of worthiness. Experience means a direct observation of or participation in events as a basis of knowledge. You have to participate with yourself. It's also important to note that healthy self-esteem is predominantly created in children by their fathers. This makes sense because it is our Heavenly Father who creates our self-esteem too. However, some people did not have healthy fathers, or they had no father figure at all. Part of developing healthy self-esteem is learning how to forgive and allow your Father in heaven to fill that deep void inside of you.

Now that you know how to be kind, compassionate, mindful, forgiving, and accepting of yourself, I hope it's easier to participate and be with yourself and others! The best way to think about self-esteem is an inward, emotional, and cognitive assessment of yourself. It is how you see yourself, it is how you respect yourself, and it is how you define your worth. You live your life through your self-esteem filter, which is why you must see yourself as God sees you!

The word "esteem" comes from the Latin word "aestimare," which means "to appraise, value, rate, weigh, estimate." Therefore, self-esteem is our cognitive and emotional praise of ourselves. More specifically, self-esteem is:

1. Confidence in your ability to think and to cope with the basic challenges of life. *Through Christ Jesus, you have amazing confidence to go through life challenges. You have everlasting mercy, grace, and His strength at your disposal.*

2. Confidence in your right to be happy, the feeling of being worthy, deserving, entitled to assert your needs and wants, and to enjoy the fruits of your efforts.

When you understand how loved you are by Christ, you learn how worthy you are! Do you see how much easier it is to have healthy and godly self-esteem when you live His way versus the world's way?

As a kid growing up without a dad and having a brother who was not too fond of me, it's fair to say I had zero self-esteem. Since I had no self-esteem, I had no boundaries, and I was so desperate for love, the wrong kind of love, I may add, that I chose to do some stupid things. I created more pain and hardship in my life and the lives of others by looking for men to admire me. Of course, my romantic relationships were not the only things to suffer. I even stayed in friendships that were unhealthy. Again, I was so desperate for connection and belonging that anyone was good enough for me. I had no standards.

I stayed with abusive, cruel, and toxic boyfriends and friends so I would not be alone. If I did not have a boyfriend, I would lock myself in my apartment, too afraid to show my face to the world. I assumed no one liked me, which only decreased my self-esteem even more so. I was so desperate to feel the love that even a toxic, unhealthy relationship was still a relationship. Perhaps you have done the same?

One time I even stayed with a boyfriend who I am pretty sure abused my oldest dog, Daisy. Admitting this pains me. It's one of my biggest regrets, and I have worked closely with the Father to learn how to forgive myself, and some days I still struggle. Unfortunately, this is what low self-esteem does.

That's the thing. The devil is hungry for great destruction and death in people's lives. I think when the devil can destroy your self-esteem, it's easier to keep you in bondage. Of course, a mini domino effect can occur too. When a person has poor self-esteem, they won't stand up for what is right, and they will allow other people and lives to be destroyed, all in the hope that a person or thing will give them what only the Father can provide!

When my husband, Austin, and I were dating, my self-esteem was better but still low. Looking back, I see how I made him my Messiah during our first few years of dating. Putting this weight on him was so unfair, and it was a large part of why our relationship was so difficult the first few years. Austin could never be what I was trying to make him, and I did not even realize I was doing it until a trusted mentor pointed it out to me. Whenever he got upset, even if I was in the right or not, I would chase after him—chasing after him only made things worse too. You see, every time he would get upset and leave, I felt I was being abandoned. I hated that feeling, so I would react by chasing after him. I believed my future was only up to me. I didn't know how to trust God or be secure in Him.

Finally, one day, I stopped chasing after him. In those times where I wanted to or was afraid, he was going to leave me, I went and prayed to God. I would say over and repeatedly, "The Lord is Messiah. I put my security in Him and not in man! He will not abandon me. He loves me unconditionally." By doing that, I learned how to trust the Father and see Him as my Messiah. By

allowing Jesus to be Lord over my life, my relationship
with Austin greatly improved!

When I was finally tired of having the victim mindset
and zero self-esteem, I found myself consistently seeking the Father's opinion of me. At that time, the Father
was not real to me the way He is to me today. However, I
borrowed other people's faith. I walked with a few people to learn more about the Father, and I knew they were
convicted of the Father's love for them. I figured, if they
had this revelation, then one day I could get it too.

It took me some time to see my worth through the
Father's eyes. It was difficult as I had to do things differently, and that was terrifying at first. One thing I
would consistently do was keep myself mentally open
with my eyes locked on the Father. I found myself talking to Him throughout the day. I invited Him into everything! I knew He would see my desire to have Him in
my life would be pure. I started to pray throughout the
day, and doing this helped me seek His opinion about
everything, which is then how I learned my will for His
kingdom. I had no idea what I was doing or how I would
see myself differently, but I trusted God. Anytime something would run through my mind that I did not like or
anytime I felt unworthy, I would call upon God. I would
recite as many verses as I knew while praying to God.

Simply having an open heart toward the Father is
a great place to start. It's incredible how the simplest

shift in focus can make the most remarkable difference. Instead of looking to man, look to God. It is easier to have confidence in yourself when you have confidence in God because you begin to care more about what He says about you and less about what you say about yourself! That may mean you need to stop idolizing a few people or things in your life. Start to see people as people, not gods, and let Jesus be Lord over your life.

The history of self-esteem is pretty interesting. Psychologist William James provided the first definition in 1892: "Self-esteem equals success divided by pretensions."[18] Meaning, feelings of self-worth come from the successes an individual achieves tempered by what the person had expected to achieve. When you expect you can do all things in Christ Jesus, amazing things happen. When you get the revelation that you can do anything in God's will for your life, it is easier to have healthy self-esteem.

For instance, if a young woman plays basketball and believes she's a good basketball player, she's more likely to put herself in situations where being a good player is important. Once she receives feedback from playing a game with friends on how she did, the feedback will determine how she feels about her basketball-playing abilities. Over time the specific instances of positive or negative feedback about her basketball playing abil-

18 Osborne, 2013.

ity will come together to create more global feelings of positive or negative self-opinion. *Now, this is why it's essential to have a victor mindset. Essentially, you allow your self-concept to be driven and enforced by the external world when you want to focus on internal validation that comes from Jesus.* Even though an individual may believe that she is a good basketball player, her ability may not live up to those expectations. She may receive feedback telling her so (for example, she may lose a game falling into a thinking trap). In this case, the individual may come to feel somewhat pessimistic about her basketball abilities. If this continues to happen, she will adjust her view of her ability and come to believe that she is not a good basketball player after all. To the extent that the person truly wanted to be good, this realization can cause her to feel quite negative and down about all aspects of herself. This is an example of low self-esteem *and how depending on external validation and poor self-talk can drain your self-esteem.*

Jesus tells us in Mark 12:31 what good self-esteem looks like.

"The second is equally important: 'Love your neighbor as yourself.' No other commandment is greater than these"
(Mark 12:31, NLT).

When you love God entirely and want to do life His way, you open yourself up to some fantastic possibilities. First, you hunger to let God's ways rule your thoughts. And when He rules your thoughts, you start to think about yourself as He does. Next, you start caring about others the way God does. You will begin finding yourself asking God what the best action is to demonstrate His love for others. In a way, you become obsessed with showing others how loved they are by the Father, making you feel better about yourself.

People with healthy self-esteem avoid negative self-talk. They also appreciate others and the natural and learned talents of others. Self-esteem means having healthy boundaries and knowing when to say "yes" or "no." Those with healthy self-esteem are self-accepting of shortcomings, limitations, and times when they fail. Instead of beating themselves up, they accept it, moving on and working to overcome it. Lastly, people with self-esteem are resilient, making it easier for them to overcome any situation through God's strength.

How Self-Esteem Is Developed

Your thoughts develop your self-esteem. I cannot stress enough to learn how to take your thoughts captive, as Paul tells us. That is why it is so critical for you to say positive things about yourself and believe them.

How do you believe something about yourself you don't necessarily feel to be true? Simple! You choose to put your faith in God and not your feelings. You let God be the God of your life instead of you! Your emotions guide you and provide information or insight, but they do not tell you what you believe. Of course, it does feel like they try too. Make the decision today to think and believe wonderful things about yourself, and if you can't, start small. Take one thing that God says about you and declare it over your life. Focus on the one attribute you like about yourself.

I remember when I was working with God to love myself as He loves me, I had to consciously think and pray to Him in the moments where I wanted to reject myself. I would tell those gremlins that my Father is powerful, and He cannot lie. What He says is the truth. Besides, who am I to not love His masterpiece?

Due to the Unloving Spirit, I was battling, and still battle at times today, I could not even look at myself in the mirror. Ugh, I hated what I looked like. However, I always thought I had nice eyes. When the gremlins would come to beat me, I would say, "I may not like that about me, but I do love my eyes. I am working with God to see myself as He sees me, and He says I am wonderfully made!" I would say this repeatedly until one day it was easier to look at myself.

Nowadays, I can look at myself with contentment. I don't like everything about myself, but I have learned that the more I walk with Christ and surrender my desires to Him, the more I can trust Him to give me my real desires. I can't tell you how many things I once desired to have emotionally, physically, or materially that I no longer care about because He changed my heart. There are also a handful of things that I now have because I stopped striving to get them out of my own will and allowed Him to give them to me if He wanted me to have them.

Another thing that has helped me is I would remind myself we are all suffering, no one is perfect, and what people say about me does not matter. It is what God says about me that matters. A few years ago, I also noticed that what I hated about myself others liked or were not bothered by. I started seeing that there was more of a spiritual component than I realized. I continued seeking God's truth in the matter through continuous and reverent prayer. He will help you walk out of whatever you are in bondage to.

Of course, other people can and will tell you their opinion of you, which can quickly get you into bondage. But, only if you come into agreement with what they say about you, their opinion does not hold a candle to God's. When someone speaks something over you, do not receive it. See those words stopping a foot away from your heart. Agreement is very, very powerful. Imagine if Eve did not come into agreement with the serpent—imagine what life would be like! Choose today to only agree with God's word, not the world.

Self-Confidence

Self-esteem is more complicated to develop than your self-confidence. But how are the two different? First, let's define self-confidence. Whereas self-esteem is inward-facing, self-confidence is outward-facing. Self-confidence is when you can successfully interact with the world around you. You can be self-confident and have low self-esteem.

The word "confidence" comes from the Latin word "*fidere*," meaning "to trust." Self-confidence means you trust yourself. This makes perfect sense, especially when you hear the signs of self-confidence, and trusting in your talents, abilities, and effort is one example. Since confidence is about trusting yourself in an area, it is no surprise that you can be confident in one area like, education, but perhaps you are not sure when it comes to your cooking skills. One awesome part about confidence is when you are unconfident in an area—if you have courage, courage will take over. Think about it this way confidence occurs when you know you are good at something, but courage is more about having the willingness and openness to try, relying on your effort, not your ability. Perhaps this is why God encourages us to be courageous amid Fear?

Let's talk about courage for a bit. Everyone has courage ingrained in them. Your level of courage can depend on your memories of when you were courageous and how they played out. It is where your self-confidence comes into play. If you were courageous and had a positive experience, there will be a known level in behaving with courage. Some people value courage and choose to respond, even when they have no idea what to do, courageously. Simply showing up with courage and relying on God's strength propels them forward.

Signs of Self-Confidence

People with healthy self-confidence appreciate and trust their abilities but place more emphasis on their effort. In the world, we call this the growth mindset. In God's kingdom, we call this trusting Him.

These individuals have developed a powerful growth mindset, meaning they know that they will get it if they try and do not give up in time. Self-confident people do not judge others, which makes sense because you treat others the way you want to be treated. We are to love our neighbors as we love ourselves; therefore, how you treat your neighbor is how you treat yourself to a degree. Confident people do their best to keep their commitments, know how to ask for help, do not feel shame, and have healthy mental flexibility and adaptability.

Choose today to appreciate the masterpiece God created you to be!

Prayer: Father God, help me to see myself as You see me. Help me to lean on Your Words and wisdom and not my own or men's. Forgive me for speaking ill about myself and not loving myself as You love me. On days where I am hating myself, I ask that you intervene. Show me how You see me. Please change my heart, allowing me to see myself as You see me! In Jesus' name, amen.

CHAPTER 14

Trusting God and Learning to Trust Yourself

Now that we have some insight into the importance of showing ourselves kindness, compassion, mindfulness, forgiveness, and acceptance, let's put it all together and help strengthen your ability to trust yourself by trusting God. Up to this point, believe it or not, we have been identifying ways to grow your trust in yourself, which allows you to hear yourself and God better. Applying kindness, compassion, mindfulness, forgiveness, and acceptance towards yourself will enable you to have a healthier relationship with yourself, which helps you trust yourself.

Many people struggle with self-doubt. The best way to describe self-doubt is not trusting yourself. Self-doubt can wreak havoc on your self-esteem and confidence because it keeps you in conflict with yourself.

God does not want you to conflict with yourself! Additionally, constantly doubting yourself causes you to be more vulnerable to the enemy's attacks.

Therefore, doubt comes from the devil.

In Genesis 3:1-4 you read the very first question in the Bible was one with the intent to instill doubt into the minds of Adam and Eve, and God did not ask this! The devil wanted them not to trust God but instead feel confused about what He said to them. In John 8:44, Jesus calls the devil "the father of lies." The devil wants to keep you in self-doubt because it is a form of bondage. If the enemy can get us to doubt God, then doubting ourselves will be that much easier.

Be sober [well balanced and self-disciplined],
be alert and cautious at all times. That enemy of yours,
the devil, prowls around like a roaring lion [fiercely hungry],
seeking someone to devour.
1 Peter 5:8 (AMP)

He wants you to doubt the truth that Jesus was both fully human and God. Once you start questioning Jesus' identity, it becomes even easier for the devil to get you to do what he wants you to do. He doesn't want you to follow Christ!

Doubt causes us to be more vulnerable to temptation. If you do not believe God is good for you and is always ready to help you, it is easier for the enemy to get you to rely on yourself in a self-righteous manner. The devil tries to persuade us to his suggestions which are always against what God wants us to do. You can help to discern if the devil is trying to trick you by asking the Holy Spirit for help, guidance, and discernment about the matter.

Secondly, you must believe and rely on God to hear you and answer your prayers. The enemy wants to bring out the critical attitude you have about the Father.

But when you ask him, be sure that your faith is in God alone. Do not waver, for a person with divided loyalty is as unsettled as a wave of the sea that is blown and tossed by the wind.

James 1:6 (NLT)

Sometimes, we can add to our self-doubt by believing we can achieve unachievable goals or expectations. The consistent failure to reach such expectations can leave anyone frustrated, confused, and doubtful of their abilities, skills, and worth. One of the biggest temptations the devil tries to do is get you to believe that you can be god. You can't. It is wise to make sure the goals you are trying to achieve first come from the Lord and second are genuinely attainable.

When you know your goals and plans are coming from the Lord, it is easier to trust yourself because God's Word says you can do all the things, He has called you to do through Him. It is God that will empower you and strengthen you to fulfill His purpose in your life. Think of it this way. You are self-sufficient in Christ's sufficiency.

However, you must not doubt God's ability to help you. In Numbers 11:21-22, we see Moses questioning God's ability to feed the wandering Israelites.

But Moses responded to the Lord, "There are 600,000 foot soldiers here with me, and yet you say, 'I will give them meat for a whole month!' Even if we butchered all our flocks and herds, would that satisfy them? Even if we caught all the fish in the sea, would that be enough?"

Numbers 11:21-22 (NLT)

The question becomes this: If Moses, who saw God's power in miracles, doubted God, how much easier is it going to be for us to doubt Him? Nonetheless, we have to choose to depend on God by using our faith completely. When you rely on your own strength and own understanding, you come to be in great danger. You must make up your mind to trust God. Here's the thing. It is hard to trust someone you do not have a strong relationship with. I encourage you to write down every time God comes through for you. This list will help you see that you can trust God and see that His strength is always available.

Additionally, look at all the people in the Bible who trusted God—look how it ended up for them! God always proves Himself to be true. He doesn't change. He doesn't lie. He is the one you need to put your trust into. When you trust Him with your life, you can rest assured that He will tell you when you are out of alignment with His will and, therefore, off track.

"For the word of the Lord holds true,
and we can trust everything he does"
(Psalm 33:4, NLT).

If that is not enough for you, then know this. That gut feeling you get that tells you to do something or not is not a fleshly feeling. It's the Holy Spirit. John 7:38 states that the Holy Spirit lives in your belly. When that sensation arises to do something or not, please pay attention to it! Remember, the Holy Spirit helps guide you to live like Christ. He dwells in you; you are the temple now. Trust yourself to discern the Holy Spirit. If you are unsure, ask for God's help and wisdom. He will help you and give you wisdom!

Additionally, negative self-talk is going to do more harm to you than good. You must start paying attention to how you internally talk to yourself. Some people are so good at speaking death over themselves that it becomes impossible for them to trust themselves because they are so busy destroying their lives with their tongue. Earlier, we identified the sounds of the gremlin, which are just evil spirits. Start to pay attention to how much time in a day you agree with those thoughts through your self-talk. It's crucial to cultivate an inner voice that responds in an intimate feeling of self-love. When you choose to speak love over yourself, it is easier to hear Jesus because He will only speak love over you.

I am the good shepherd; I know my own sheep,
and they know me, just as my Father knows me and
I know the Father. So I sacrifice my life for the sheep.
I have other sheep, too, that are not in this sheepfold.
I must bring them also. They will listen to my voice, and there
will be one flock with one shepherd.
John 10:14-16 (NLT)

Positive Self-Talk

Positive self-talk, trusting yourself, and trusting God all go hand-in-hand. Think about it. Do you listen or trust people who speak negatively to you? No, you don't, and the same will be true for yourself. Plus, there is a massive problem with negativity. The more negativity you speak and hear, the more you focus and filter in negativity.

One reason for negative self-talk is you are personalizing, usually with an over-emphasis. You blame yourself the second things go wrong. Doesn't this sound like the victim mindset we discussed earlier? Before you immediately blame yourself, practice mindfulness by asking a few questions, but first, invite the Father in to help with your ability to discern. *Was this really my fault?* Sometimes you may be at fault, but compassion reminds us that we are not perfect. We are going to make mistakes, which is when we apply self-acceptance and kindness. I then encourage you to ask yourself, *What could I have done better or different? If it's not your fault, ask yourself: What makes me blame myself for something that is out of my control? What can I learn from this experience?*

I believe there is always something to learn. You sometimes have to look at the situation with glasses that help you identify any blessing or lesson, which requires God's help.

The second reason is that you polarize the situation. Remember that all-or-nothing thinking trap, and how much of life is a broad grayscale? When you view a situation as either good or bad, successful or failure, you have left no room for the reality of life, which is typically a gray area. Again, take this time as an opportunity for growth. Reflection with the assistance of God is the fastest way to emotional and spiritual maturity. Ask God to help you identify where you could improve.

Remember, nothing can take away your self-worth. You may fail. You may make some royally stupid decisions, but you are still worthy. Forgive yourself and ask God to forgive you as well.

The third reason is that you magnify your situation and allow the gremlin or spirits to have a field day. If you look hard enough, you can honestly find a blessing amid everything. It might be as small as a mustard seed or as large as an elephant, but there is a blessing in everything. You have to look for it. When we magnify a situation, we typically only focus on the negative aspects and neglect the blessings, especially when our self-talk is mainly negative. The reality is there is no benefit to this perspective. You are thinking in a problem-focused manner which will only keep you stuck. The more you think and speak negatively, the more you train your brain to make this your default system. When you notice your focus is on the negative, I want you to ask yourself, what are the blessings in this situation? Again, ask for the Father's help with this. Also, be patient. Sometimes it takes some time before you see the fruit of the blessing come to pass.

Lastly, we catastrophize the situation, which causes us to prepare for the worst. We dismiss the potential for our faith to be put into action. We force God out of the equation. No one enjoys the company of those people. You might love them as we should, but they are not delightful to be around. Well, neither are you when you do the same.

Remember, your brain will do what you tell it to, even if you are unaware. Our brains will work to create what we most think about, which is why choosing to trust yourself and speak positively about yourself is so important. However, it would help if you had a focus other than yourself. The more you think about yourself, the more you focus on yourself, the more miserable you will become. It's a fine line. You want to acknowledge yourself and your needs, but you don't want to focus only on yourself because you do not live a satisfying life when you do. Why? Simple, you have taken your focus and trust away from God. Only the Father can satisfy you in the way you are desiring and searching to be satisfied.

We know this to be true when therapists encourage depressed people to volunteer. By default, when we focus on helping other people, we help ourselves. If you do not have a purpose higher than yourself, you will be in trouble. Again, you are a spirit. You have a soul, and you live in a body. Ignoring your spiritual needs, which is a relationship with the Father, causes you to ignore your existence and true purpose. God created you for Him. He wants you to serve Him, and the results are life-changing. Your spiritual component is a high priority. God wired our brains to believe in Him. *Neurotheology has proven that the moment you encounter God, your brain begins to change. The University of Pennsylvania Neurotheology Research team has proven God to be part of our consciousness. Thinking about God alters your neural circuitry in specific parts of your brain, which is proof that God can renew your brain. Additionally, this team proved the unique construction of the human brain perceives and generates spiritual realities.*[19] Did you know that neurotheology has also confirmed that every human being contemplates the existence of the spiritual realm starting at an early age?

"Only fools say in their hearts, 'There is no God.' They are corrupt, and their actions are evil; not one of them does good" (Psalm 53:1, NLT).

If you believe in God and know He is good and loves you, then your feelings towards yourself will be kinder, tender, and more compassionate than if you don't believe in anything. Sociologists have found that teens who attend regular religious services have years in religious youth groups and view faith as highly important are associated with higher self-esteem and more positive self-attitudes. If this benefits teens, then it can also aid in adults' lives. In addition, those who believe in God understand God created them for a specific

19 Newberg & Waldman, 2009.

purpose. People who understand they have a particular God-given purpose will focus on fulfilling that purpose.

We all need a purpose. It helps move us forward when we feel we cannot. You need to live for God because living for God empowers you to keep going even when you think you cannot.

One thing that has helped me destroy negative thinking, other than consciously contemplating on Philippians 4:8, is I chose to uphold Ephesians 4:29. It's crazy what will happen to you when the Holy Spirit makes a verse come to life for you. While I am not perfect at this, I do my best with God's help not to allow any corrupt communications out of my mouth (Ephesians 4:29). When I surround myself with loved ones and friends, I also let them know I will not speak nor listen to corrupt communication. I also focus on not talking ill or gossiping about someone. If I wouldn't say it to their face, why am I saying it to someone else's face?

"So encourage each other and build each other up"
(1 Thessalonians 5:11a, NLT).

Benefits of Positive Self-Talk

Additionally, positive self-talk without a relationship with God will help decrease anxiety and stress, increase resilience, boost confidence, and builds healthier relationships. That is without the help of God. Imagine how many more benefits there are when doing it God's way.

Father God, help me to trust You in every area of my life. I want a strong relationship with You. I open myself up entirely to You and Your ways. Teach me; mold me; direct me. Change my heart only to want to live for You and help me trust You completely. In Jesus' name, amen.

CHAPTER 15

Trials and Tribulations

---

*Dear brothers and sisters, when troubles of any
kind come your way, consider it an opportunity for
great joy. For you know that when your faith is tested,
your endurance has a chance to grow.*

James 1:2-3 (NLT)

Trials and tribulations are going to happen to you
for the rest of your life! I promise you this. I can only
guarantee that you will face a handful of realities, and
experiencing trials and tribulations is one of those!
Trials and tribulations are another way of saying suffering will happen to you. You will sometimes experience hardships, emotional pain, internal struggles, and
other obstacles that you will label as challenging. That's
okay. You can view the trials and tribulations that attack
you in two lights: *why me?* Or *as an opportunity to grow*

and become stronger. Part of living as a victor means you change your perception of difficult seasons.

The victim mindset wants to grovel, complain, and agree with Fear when hardships occur. Typically, they want to avoid the pain and hide, doing nothing about it. Rarely do they want to grab the bull by the horn, being proactive, nor embrace the experience. However, victors see these seasons as an opportunity to profit from, grow, and strengthen their character. Ultimately suffering helps build our endurance and patience.

"We can rejoice, too, when we run into problems and trials, for we know that they help us develop endurance"
(Romans 5:3, NLT).

No, difficult seasons are not fun, per se. While everyone faces these challenging times, I am not encouraging you to fake your way through it with a pretend smile on your face. Instead, I am encouraging you to see this as an opportunity for great joy. If you can start to see suffering as an opportunity to become better and stronger for God's kingdom, it is easier to face such hardships with a positive outlook. Additionally, you may not resist such seasons because you start to see that everyone suffers, so it's not a personal attack. It's a shared reality.

As you navigate your own suffering and transform your thinking into that of a victor, do not forget that we live in a fallen world. Since this is our reality, you must understand that good behavior and righteous living do not always end in a reward. Similarly, bad behavior is sometimes rewarded instead of punished. The reality is that sin has twisted our world, creating an unpredictable, ruthless, and ugly reality. Stop fighting this and start accepting while understanding that Jesus has already overcome the world.

If you struggle to accept suffering is a part of your life, and good things can come from it, I encourage you to read the story of Job. God is faithful, and you can trust Him in every season and every aspect of your life.

Why Suffering Occurs

Trials and tribulations occur for a handful of reasons. For instance, sin in one's life, lack of or weak faith, the reality of living in a fallen world, attacks from the devil, and even living an effective life. Sometimes God will protect you from suffering, stopping it from being a reality in your life, and other times He will allow you to face it. Understand that God is still with you even amid suffering, and He alone can help you overcome it.

Let's examine a few reasons why suffering occurs:

1. Suffering can encourage us to depend more on Him!

2. Suffering can help us become humbler before God and man.

3. Suffering can be a sign of faithful Christian living. Sometimes obeying God leads to suffering because the world hates Him and His followers. Jesus suffered because of His love for us. You, too, can experience suffering when you selflessly help someone else.

4. Suffering helps develop an eternal perspective, allowing you to see what matters in life.

5. Suffering helps you draw closer to God. It can be easy to start to delete God from your life. The Philistines witnessed great victory from the Father over their god, Dagon. They did not surrender their life to the Father until after they were burdened with tumors. Sometimes it takes experiencing pain before you allow God into your life.

6. Suffering can help you destroy your fake faith and increase your faith.

7. Suffering is not always a result of sin.

8. Suffering can be a result of listening to your flesh as opposed to staying in the Spirit.

9. Suffering can be a result of another person's foolishness.

10. Suffering can sometimes be because you are personally getting attacked by evil spirits.

There are so many things that lead one to experience suffering. Sometimes it is easier to discern, and other times it is ambiguous as to why. While suffering will happen and doesn't feel good, it can create some fantastic blessings!

Benefits of Suffering

Jesus experienced great suffering, and as a result of His suffering, we have salvation! Truthfully, He could have saved Himself, but He chose to face suffering because of how much He loves us! His love for us and willingness to endure is why our sins are forgiven because He paid the ultimate price!

While it is so easy to believe the lies that suffering sucks and nothing good will come from it, know that is just a lie. There are so many wonderful possibilities that come because of suffering. As a victor, it is important to focus on the truth-understanding you are not forsaken and that God redeems.

Have you ever noticed that some of the people in the world with the greatest characters are those who experienced tremendous suffering?

Suffering is one way that can create character in ourselves. There is a misbelief today that if you are experiencing suffering, it is due to you doing life or an area of your life incorrectly (Job's friends said this too). But, as we learned from the Bible will all face suffering.

Paul tells us in 1 Corinthians 13:13 that faith, hope, and love will last forever! Notice these three things are the heart of the Christian lifestyle! God uses the devil's attacks to help build our character in those three areas. The more problems you have, the more perseverance you will develop. When you are persistent about doing life God's way, your character will strengthen to be more like Christ's, which then helps you trust God in a greater way. When you trust God with your life, it is easier to trust Him with your future because you will know He only wants to give you good plans for your life and help increase your hope!

Suffering also helps you see if you are living by Christ's values or not. It is easy to say you read the Bible and believe in Jesus, but what happens when your life becomes hard? Suffering helps test your values, showcasing if what you believe is what you claim. The truth is you cannot grow from calm seasons like you can from difficult ones. In times of suffering, what do you do? Do you turn to God, or do you turn to yourself?

Suffering helps us increase our faith in God! Sometimes suffering is not a punishment but an opportunity from God for you to prove your loyalty to Him. Victors understand to live is Christ and to die is gain (Philippians 1:21). Therefore, victors are always ready to face death for the cause of Christ. Are you? If you are not, that is okay. Talk to God about it. He will help you grow your faith.

Suffering can bring rewards. Instead of focusing on the pains of suffering, focus on all the good God can bring as a result. He is a redeemer!

Suffering can help you see where your human limitations are. While many of us do not like to admit that we have limitations and weaknesses, these aspects of our human makeup can empower us to develop the attributes to emulate Christ. It is through our humanism that God can display His power. Paul learned that His strength and grace were sufficient in times of his weakness. It is through recognizing the frailty of our humanism that we hunger to depend more on God!

What if I told you that suffering is a huge privilege? Would that change your opinion on it? Suffering can enable you to represent Christ faithfully! As your eyes will naturally start to shift from earthly comforts, superficial belief, all while strengthening your faith and encouraging others to bear their cross for Christ. When we hear others holding on to their belief in Christ amid extreme suffering, our faith is increased, and we can become more inspired to live our lives for Him!

Lastly, suffering can help you become more like Christ! As believers, we are to want to become more like Christ in every way! We need to be willing to move when God says move regardless of what we may face.

Those who suffer and still faithfully obey God have won a tremendous battle over their sinful nature! This victory tells us about such people that sin can start to lose its power over us, but only if we choose to keep our eyes on Jesus!

Navigating Suffering

Of course, sometimes it is easier said than done. Here are a few things you can do to help you renew your mind in the parameters of suffering.

What are some things you can consciously do with the help of the Holy Spirit to see suffering in a different light? Well, first, become mindfully aware of where your focus goes when suffering comes to your door! Where you put your focus is where you will put your trust. The only way to battle anything in life is through keeping your eyes on Jesus!

Keeping Your Eyes on Jesus

Do you know what most people do when they start to experience trials and tribulations?

They keep their eyes focused on the storm, tribulation, suffering, or the giant in the situation. Essentially, they are focused on what they can see. They allow their carnal mind to take charge, causing them to go by sight, not faith. When you exclude Jesus from the equation, you fall out of the Spirit and into the flesh, which is sin in itself. However, Paul clarifies we are to go by faith and not by sight (2 Corinthians 5:7). As the only way to please God is with faith (Hebrews 11:6).

When you focus on the problem of the matter, you stumble and turn away from God. Even if you do not realize it, you tell God that you would rather depend on your own resources than trust in Him. And that, my dear friend, is self-righteous! It's just like what Max Lucado says, "Focus on giants—you stumble. Focus on God—giants tumble!" The only way for you to rise in a storm is by focusing and believing in God's promises, not your circumstances.

Jesus tells His disciples in John 16:33 (NLT), "I have told you all this so that you may have peace in me. Here on earth you will have many trials and sorrows. But take heart, because I have overcome the world."

It seems people forget the last sentence in this verse. I cannot begin to tell you how many pastors I have heard use this verse in discussing resilience and the truth that hardship will come to you, but they always leave out that last part. The most important part of the verse is where He promises peace and has already overcome the world. Yes, on earth, you will have trials and sorrow, but take heart because Jesus has overcome the world—this is what you need to rest on! Keep your eyes on Jesus and allow His peace to enter your heart.

Jesus tells us to take courage in Him because He has overcome the world. Do you see the victory in this truth? If Jesus is part of the Godhead and the Holy Spirit is the greatest power to exist, do you see how victorious you are when you choose to remain in Him? "Remain in me, and I will remain in you. For a branch cannot produce fruit if it is severed from the vine, and you cannot be fruitful unless you remain in me" (John 15:4, NLT).

What Jesus is telling you in John 15:4 is that you are to make constant, moment-by-moment decisions to follow Jesus. You cannot be passive about this. You must be proactive! That is why the Word reminds you so many times to keep your eyes focused on Him, which is what victors do!

You must remember, when the devil is trying to bring you down—he has already lost because Jesus has already overcome the world. It's done. Jesus overcame the world by rising from the grave. Rest on that truth instead of getting caught up in the lies the devil is trying to sell you, typically through Fear.

I, too, sometimes get overwhelmed by suffering, buying the lie that my life will be ruined! Understand that your life's purpose cannot be destroyed by suffering when you trust in Jesus. You were put on this earth for a relationship with the Father, not to experience material possessions. If you do die as the result of suffering, you will go to heaven! That is extraordinary when you truly trust God.

Here is the thing. It can be effortless to fall into self-pity, catastrophizing, or even make presumptuous conclusions about the situation. All of this is part of the victims' mindset amid suffering. If you do, that's okay, but catch yourself, repent, and ask God to help you not fall into such thought patterns again.

Victory Amid the Pain

Maintaining a victor's way of thinking amid suffering means you must understand the beauty amid the pain. Learn how to rejoice when you are suffering. Allow God to be your joy, not circumstances or humanly sensations. We will experience unnecessary suffering by following Jesus. I delight in those moments where I am persecuted! The Bible tells us too. Plus, we are to be like Christ in everything. He rejoiced and gladly endured His suffering, so shouldn't I do the same?

The movie *Passion of the Christ* provides a small glimpse of what Jesus went through. It is a movie that encouraged me to fight the good fight. Perhaps it helped your faith too. While that movie is always brutal for me to watch, it's said that director Mel Gibson could not portray the violence and torture Jesus endured because it would have fallen outside the rating requirements. That says so much to me. It is a powerful movie. I encourage you to watch it.

Since Jesus has gone through extreme suffering, He will help you endure your suffering too. You can trust Jesus to empower you to survive and overcome all suffering and temptation. Instead of complaining, letting Fear consume you, go to Jesus and ask for His help and patience!

I have learned to ingrain in my mind that suffering is a wonderful opportunity for me to grow, rejoice, thank the Father, and allow Him to be glorified. Yes, suffering might be painful and uncomfortable. Still, like everything, I remind myself; eventually, the pain will pass, and I will be better, wiser, and stronger as a result. When I look back to all the hardships of my childhood, I know I was once bitter about it all. However, when I allowed Jesus to take them from me, He took the memories too, but not the lessons. What I learned is there is a tremendous benefit to experiencing suffering. I am grateful for what I endured because it has empowered me to share the Gospel and God's power, and that is priceless! Sometimes it takes making a mistake before we can learn to trust the more excellent way that is found in Christ.

Emotional setbacks can result from not developing the mental ability (perseverance) to deal with a new set of problems. Neurologically speaking, you are at the limit of your neural pathways, and your brain does not know what to do. But, once you face those setbacks and overcome them, your ability to endure grows greater, which is why setbacks are opportunities for growth, not defeat.

If you can remember, this is an open invitation for you to grow and improve yourself in moments of sorrow. You allow the possibility of a joyous victory and encouragement that will continue to propel you forward in the name of Christ. Just like athletes have to train to get better and develop strong self-discipline and physical discipline, you must train your minds for a mental race of endurance. Think about it; things that once hurt your feelings as a kid that no longer offend you are because you have taken that opportunity to grow. You understand now why Sally did not invite you to her birthday party that you did not as a kid. For instance, as a kid, you heard "birthday party" and thought "fun," omitting the truth that you and Sally were not friends.

Giving yourself time to mindfully reflect, practice the components of love, and spend time praying to God will help you see a new light on every situation. Give everything to God and ask Him what He wants you to do and how He wants you to respond!

Prayer: Father God, thank You for saving me. Thank You for loving me so much that You allowed Your Son to endure such hardships. In times of suffering and pain, Father, help me to keep my eyes focused on You and not the problem. Allow me to see these moments as tremendous opportunities and courageously forge ahead instead of coward away. Father, please use me in any way You see fit. Allow me to glorify You in everything, even if I do not understand. Father, help me to see that Your strengthen is most sufficient in my weakness and help me to trust You in everything.

CHAPTER 16

Emotional Intelligence

Many of us allow our emotions to drive and dictate us as opposed to us controlling our emotions. Many people will tell you that you should go by your feelings. However, taking your emotions as truth can be damaging. Please remember the devil will try to reach you through your carnal mind, which consists of your senses.

I think we have lost focus on what emotions truthfully tell us, which is why I want to take some time to clarify how we can leverage our feelings. The reality is you can control your mind, or your mind will control you. One of the first things you need to do to learn to gain control over your flesh is by continuously asking the Father, "What do You want me to do?" When the Holy Spirit responds to you, obediently follow through with the command.

*"So letting your sinful nature control your mind
leads to death. But letting the Spirit control your
mind leads to life and peace"*
(Romans 8:6, NLT).

Emotions are the physical, gut-felt responses that fuel our behavior and motivate us to act. Emotions allow life to be more engaging, exciting, and less dull. In relationships, it is your emotions that inspire you to seek closeness during times of stress. Emotions bring color to the world. Like anything, you have to learn how to respond and navigate your emotions because they tell you much information. Think of emotions like your car's dashboard. When a light comes on, like check tire pressure, it alerts you to put more pressure in your tires. Essentially, the light tells you that your tire pressure could be low, or it could be a miswiring in the car's computer system. Nonetheless, it gives us insight into the internal workings of the vehicle.

Your emotions do the same. They provide insight into your being. However, it's essential for you to understand, as I have said already, that you are a spirit. You have a mind or soul, and you live in a body. When your emotions are popping up, you need to do a mindful inspection of yourself.

For instance, if you are stressed and irritable, you will respond with shortness, and you may hyperfocus on the stressful event and distance yourself from your loved ones. If you are reacting like this, it's fair to say you have agreed with the kingdom of darkness, not God! Instead of beating yourself up, quickly repent recalibrating yourself to God's kingdom.

Your emotions help alert you to what is going on and what needs to be handled inside your body. Now, it's dangerous when you allow your body's emotions to dictate your entire life. Life is about choices. If you are waiting to feel motivated or feel love, forgiveness, joy, or angry before you do something, you are allowing your emotions to dictate you.

The truth is if right now you screamed, "*I have joy, yes, I do. I have joy, joy, joy. I am joyful; yes, I am!*" your body would respond to what you are telling it. Especially if you said it enough until you smiled, laughing, wondering if you were crazy or not.

Some people allow their emotions to create their habits. Some may be great habits, and others might be adding more suffering to their world.

Regularly checking in with yourself is how you grow your awareness and can mindfully observe what is going on, which can help you identify the real root. It's not until you become aware of your behaviors through your emotions that you can catch them, challenge them, and determine what the triggers are. Therefore, until we can identify these triggers, the habits motivated by feelings will dictate and control how you perceive and react to situations. Remember, your perception can be wrong!

Neuroscience reveals that we have a critical choice point, and it is my experience that you can grow this critical choice point. It is like this magic moment or magic second that happens right before, making the decision to either reject or agree with the thought. We always have a choice, even when we feel we do not.

Hindsight is a powerful tool. God wants us to be reflective individuals, seeking Him in all things. An example of leveraging hindsight is taking some time to think about your choices after a situation consciously. You then ask yourself how you could have handled the situation better and chosen to respond to the information instead of reacting? Again, invite God into this process. Also, use a friend, therapist, or coach as a sounding board to help you process or see different perspectives. When you take time to think of all the ways you could have successfully done it, you strategize and plant bright, godly seeds. Now, there will be times where you have to plant those seeds a few times before they will grow. Even the Bible speaks to this!

As a child, one of my favorite things to do was journal. I believe that because I was so passionate about journaling, my awareness of myself has grown. Now, I ask God to show me every incident where I failed to respond in a godly manner. I also ask Him to show me what is the better way to have responded. You see, I am hungry to learn how to do everything God's way. Of course, I mess up a lot, which only helps aid in my learning.

It is your focus on God and your decision to persevere that will get you there.

Becoming aware of emotional patterns gives you insight into where your misbeliefs are. When you can identify limiting beliefs, you can then work to change them. It is hard to make improvements in areas where you don't know you need to improve.

In our darker moments and most upsetting feelings, we have an opportunity for spiritual growth and to uncover the Father's wisdom. Psychologists believe strong emotions are messages from the unconscious. When you take time to explore what is causing emotion to be so intense with the help of God, you can begin to learn some tremendous insight. In turn, you can learn how to be better prepared and not repurchase the lies.

When we get caught up in our emotions, we can forget many truths about God, which causes us to forget God's character. Learning how to discern and better understand what is driving your emotions can help you emulate Christ better. Jesus was always in control emotionally. He exemplified great discipline, focus, and control over His flesh. The truth is your emotions can lie to you! Instead of agreeing with every sensation you feel, become more curious.

Additionally, sometimes the Christian community puts down emotions, making them seem as if they are bad. Understand emotions are not bad. God encourages us to express our emotions and not hold them in. He would rather you go to Him upset and angry at Him than try to keep it from Him. When you keep your unresolved emotions inside, your body is affected for the worst. God has given us a full range of emotions.

Your brain has automatic responses in situations when triggered. These automatic responses can be from generational choices or your brain learning how you consistently respond to something. Sometimes we can be afraid of things that we do not need to fear. When this happens, our brain will think we are gearing up to fight a saber-tooth tiger.

There are times where investigating your emotions is necessary. When your brain has walked down the same neural pathway a handful of times, it becomes your brain's default mode when that stimulus appears. Think about it this way. That synaptic nerve that tells your brain to respond the way you do has been walked upon so much that it becomes the default path. The best way you can envision what I am talking about is to see your default neural pathways as the same as a hiking trail that has been walked upon millions of times.

If you have ever gone hiking before, take a second to envision those trails. Usually, the millions of people who have walked upon the trail have beaten the ground down, making the trail quite noticeable and reasonably easy to follow. The dominant course is easier to walk on compared to if you decided to make your own trail. Therefore, if you did choose to walk off the compacted path, it would most likely take more effort and time to walk along. Now, if you started to walk off the track and walked the same new path repeatedly, it would slowly become beaten down and, in time, easier to walk. The same is true for our neural pathways. At some point, you have to choose to practice responding differently.

Take a second to do the exercise below. First, read the scenario, then identify how you currently respond. Next, identify and imagine how you would prefer to answer.

When I feel attacked, I...

When someone buys me a gift or compliments me, I...

When I tell myself I am not good enough, I...

When someone hurts my feelings or does something I don't like, I...

When someone educates me about something I feel I should know, I...

Use the exercise above to think and imagine yourself responding in a new way. As you image yourself responding in this new way, focus on that magical moment before your brain decides which synaptic nerve to ride. Enhance that magic moment and get familiar with catching that moment and choosing a better way to respond.

God + You

We are working to develop healthy vulnerability, which is required to be in a healthy relationship. Vulnerability is the core aspect of spirituality. You are relinquishing control of your life to a greater being that you know you can fully always trust and has your back. When you are aware of your needs and that you are a spirit and your spirit has needs and how short life is and how you were created to be vulnerable, you become more open to a relationship with God. Now in Chapter 4, Attachment Theory, we talked about relationship styles. I am going to refer back to them because we are called to be in a relationship with God. However, if we operate in relationships in an unhealthy manner, we will carry the same tendencies to God, and we are hurting ourselves when we do this. I have been and still am guilty in these areas. But, we want to focus more on leaving where we are, not arriving; it's a journey.

A secure relationship style, one that is healthy, will cry out to God and pray for the answer they are looking for, and they believe in their core that all things work for the greater good. God will never forsake you or abandon you. Now, we were created to be in a relationship with God and man. However, your relationship with God should be your primary focus, but you do need other relationships. Isolation is dangerous because it is how evil spirits can get to you. Think about secrets. When we feel we cannot tell anyone something because of how a person might react, we are isolated. Secure relationship style also understands God's love is stronger than death. Nothing can separate you.

I do not know how someone can live in this world without a spiritual source. When I was younger, I was not as close to God as I am now, but I wish I had been. God's kingdom provides refuge for our souls in times of trouble. He is your safe haven. Now, this is important. God is always with you! Even when you do not feel Him, which is why I talked to you about not allowing your emotions to dictate your life. I have learned in moments where I no longer feel God, it's because I stepped away from God. He didn't step away from me, but I stepped out from His umbrella. So, what do I do? I go back to the last place I knew I was connected to God in my life, and I think about what steps I took along the way that may have gotten me off course. I repent and move forward.

Now, insecure people handle a relationship with God quite differently. The avoidant style keeps people at a distance, which is no surprise that this individual moves away from God and clings to possessions, success, or addictions in moments of stress. Sometimes they even feel anger towards God and even believe they cannot trust God. It is not true. It's all lies. You were created to have fellowship with God, and He can take all that fear from you if you give it to Him. He wants to free you. The anxious relationship style concerns rejection and abandonment, which is why they typically do not turn to God for comfort but addictions or focus on their successes. The disorganized relationship style bounces back and forth between the relationship styles of avoidance and anxious, but they cry a continual story of loss. They tend to see God as malicious, but we know deep down, and these individuals know too, that He is the opposite. God is love.

I wanted to go over this to help you see some commonalities with all your relationships. I believe God does the impossible. I have seen God and His word save my life multiple times. I would not view trials and tribulation the way I do if it were not for Him. Your relationship style and your misbeliefs will impact your relationship with God. I promise to have a successful life and to be a whole individual; God must be number one.

"Be strong and courageous, for you are the one who will lead these people to possess all the land I swore to their ancestors I would give them. Be strong and very courageous. Be careful to obey all the instructions Moses gave you. Do not deviate from them, turning either to the right or to the left. Then you will be successful in everything you do. Study this Book of Instruction continually. Meditate on it day and night so you will be sure to obey everything written in it. Only then will you prosper and succeed in all you do. This is my command—be strong and courageous! Do not be afraid or discouraged. For the Lord your God is with you wherever you go."
Joshua 1:6-9 (NLT)

Limbic System

Let's talk a bit about our brain. I am going to quickly talk about the limbic system of our brain to hopefully help put a few things in perspective for you. Sometimes understanding allows for greater awareness to occur.

The limbic system is responsible for categorizing, interpreting, and sorting sensory input, filtering billions of bits of information we experience at any given moment, determining how we will code the data, and how we will respond, and it stores memories, regulate hormones, and is involved in motor function.[20] Your

---

20 Hopper, 2018.

limbic system is your first response system. When you quickly react, you are in your limbic system.

The brain has an infinite ability to protect itself. When we fell, our brain went from its natural solution-focused and Christ-minded state of mind to surviving when Adam ate the forbidden fruit. Our brain went from thriving to surviving. Therefore, I believe when you get out of your carnal mind, learn to operate in your Spirit Man, you can quickly find solutions because God created our mind to be solution-focused, to thrive. Now, of course, let us not forget that God is all-knowing. Jesus said, if you have seen me, you have seen the Father (John 14:9). Since Jesus was both fully human and God, and we have the mind of Christ (1 Corinthians 2:16), we have one extraordinary brain!

The location of the limbic brain is primarily in the midbrain. It filters and sorts one billion bits of sensory information internally and externally in your environment.[21] The brain categorizes the data as either safe or unsafe, usually based off past experiences or your beliefs, which is why your body reacts to worry.

We all are familiar with the dangers of stress, not just to our bodies but to our minds. Dr. Caroline Leaf (2013) has defined stress as "a condition typically characterized by symptoms of mental, physical tension, or strain

---

21 Hopper, 2018.

as depression, hypertension that can result from a reaction in which a person feels threatened or pressured."[22]

God is our Father in heaven. He is our protector; He wants us to not worry (stress) because of how damaging stress is to our bodies. Worry will steal and destroy (John 10:10) your life, memories, and health from you. When you're worrying, you're participating with the enemy.

Concern motivates while worry paralyzes you.

A simple example of this would be if you saw a young toddler banging their head on a wall, knowing it would hurt them, you would get them to stop. You would not want them to participate in potentially harmful behavior because you know how damaging trauma can be to the brain. The same is true for our Heavenly Father. When you join worry, you are participating in harmful behaviors that are stealing life from you. He wants to stop you from riding on the merry-go-round of worry because of the potential harm it causes, but He will only intervene but so much because He gave you a god-like power, free will. You may not realize it, but free will is a powerful and god-like characteristic. You can decide and make choices, which is what God did, and therefore it is powerful. Since you have free will, you have to choose to surrender those worries and stresses to God and focus on Him, bringing you joy, peace, and life.

---

22 Dr. Caroline Leaf, p. 36.

A limbic loop is a limbic system injury. It is where a person is caught in a flight, fight, freeze response; a person is always on guard, ready to protect him or herself. Usually, such injury occurs through chronic stress, trauma, childhood abuse, seeing your parents worry, PTSD, etc.[23] Now, not all limbic loops are due to such severity. If you cannot stop thinking about how you will pay your bills or if you are one of those people who are worrying about your child's well-being five hours a day, you are in a limbic loop. People who experience Obsessive-Compulsive Disorder (OCD) are in a limbic loop.[24] People who obsess about their weight or are triggered by smells are also suffering a limbic loop injury. Most of us do or have experienced one at one time or another. Understand spiritually speaking, all this comes out of a place where you do not feel good about yourself. Essentially it is the Unloving Spirit stealing life from you! The spirit gets you believing that you should obsess over your flaws, constantly working to change them to receive love. Notice you are driven by Fear to change and not by love.

Please remember that you might have a limbic system injury or impairment, but the truth is you were healed by His stripes (1 Peter 2:24). The goal of breaking your limbic loops is to get your Spirit Man controlling

23 Hopper, 2018.

24 Hopper, 2018.

your body, instead of your body controlling your spirit, allowing the healing of your limbic loop to manifest in your body. Also, I hope you learn how to surrender your worries and start listening to your Spirit Man.

If you experience the same or similar thoughts play in your mind on repeat, then you have experienced a limbic loop. If you have worried about the same matter multiple times, then you have experienced a limbic loop. It's time to stop it and do the more excellent way!

If God has overcome the world, don't you think He can overcome your problems too?

Of course, He can! You must get your thoughts renewed to a higher way of thinking, which is only found in Christ. I promise if you think like Christ, you are thinking better, which means you feel better. You can do this. Now, let's do this!

Before I began repairing my limbic system, I was very allergic to fragrances. I could not stand to be around perfume, floral scents of any kind because I would get a sore throat and a migraine. Then I started learning about the limbic system and how to retrain it. I added some of my own components, and within two weeks, I was utterly free of reactions to smells. This is the power of doing things God's way. It's quite common for children who have experienced abuse to develop Multiple Chemical Sensitivity, but we are healed again through Christ's suffering! I am not too fond of perfumes and prefer not to use scented formulas, but I no longer get terrible migraines and sore throats when around scents. Victory! And victory is yours too. You need to retrain your thinking and take authority over your body by using the authority Christ has given you!

What I find ironic, and I speak from experience because I was in a limbic loop for years, is the person's attention is on carnal matters, worldly matters, and is focusing much attention on time. All things that God tells us to not focus on!

> *"Set your mind on things above, not on things on the earth"* (Colossians 3:2, NKJV).

The worries, anxieties, financial issues, or whatever you are facing currently will fade the more you trust God with your life. That is a promise. I also promise you other "problems" will come too. However, compared to eternity, your carnal and worldly problems are a blip on the radar.

Prayer: Father God, please help me respond as You would have me respond in every situation. Please help me to resemble Jesus' emotional intelligence. Please highlight my weak areas and help me lean on You to respond more appropriately. Show me how to live from my spirit and not from my carnal mind. In everything I do, show me how I can live for You! In Jesus' name, amen.

CHAPTER 17

Getting to Know Your Authentic Self

Who Are You

Who are you? Think about that question for a second. The question "Who are you?" is a short question that holds a significant punch! It's a question that encompasses an extensive and detailed answer. It's a question that starts a domino effect of more questions, like *"What makes me, me?"* Or *"what makes me tick, excited, focused, annoyed?"* Or *"what makes me a human?"* Or *"what makes me unique?"* Or *"what truths make me uniquely me and won't change?"* These additional questions are fantastic to be asking yourself whether you're aware you are asking them or not. See, most of us struggle to answer that question because we do not take the time to investigate who we are. Most people allow what they do and experience to define them as oppose to who they are, which causes one to emphasize the doing versus the being.

As you think about how you would answer the question, *"Who am I?"* The first few things that come up might be connected to what you do or have.

But that does not answer the question of who are you? What you do is not and will never be who you are. How you behave is not who you are either.

What if I told you who you are is who God says you are? Your truest, most authentic self is who God designed you to be, which is why it is so satisfying!

Maybe you have been defining who you are by some of your traumas or where you currently are in life and rejecting what God says about you. Well, now it's time to get recalibrated to the truth.

I was about twenty-three years old when I was first asked this question! I could not answer it. Every time I tried, I described a doing, not a being. I quickly grew frustrated and scared because I saw I had no idea who I was. It took me spending some time on a game reserve in South Africa before I finally realized who I was. A child of God! Prior to having this revelation, I was constantly searching for satisfaction, comfort, and security in all the wrong places. Before I committed my life to God, I did things my way. I had no idea what my purpose was, and I had no idea what God could do. I was lost and tried it my way, which did not work. I will tell you when you claim the truth (God's Word) over the facts of your life, your life changes.

For instance, when you define who you are, it's essential to focus on what God says about you because that truth will never change. Now, since we are created in God's image, we know from that we are and have some tremendous power in us, which is why the phrase "I am" is so powerful, as you will learn in the next section. My theory is this. If I am a spirit, and I have a mind, and I live in a body, then to accurately answer the question, "Who am I?" My answer must be more spirit-focused than soul or body-based. Now your response will still encompass your mind and body because we have them and engage with our minds, souls, and bodies daily. Below is a list of some things God says about you:

- I am a child of the light and the day (1 Thessalonians 5:5).
- I am a new creation in Him (2 Corinthians 5:17).
- God loved me before He made the whole word (Ephesians 1:4).
- I am righteous and holy (Ephesians 4:24).
- I have been born again by the Holy Spirit (John 3:3-6).
- Christ's blood is why I am healed and forgiven (Ephesians 4;1; 1 Peter 2:24).
- I have the mind of Christ (1 Corinthians 2:16).
- I have the peace of God (Philippians 4:7).

- I am strengthened through God (Philippians 4:13).
- I am God's workmanship (Ephesians 2:10).
- I am greatly loved (John 3:16; Ephesians 2:4; Colossians 3:12; 1 Thessalonians 1:4).
- I am fearless (2 Timothy 1:7).
- I radiate light wherever I go (Matthew 5:1).
- God sees me without fault in His eyes (Ephesians 1:4).
- God showers kindness, wisdom, and understanding on me (Ephesians 1:8).

Above is just a tasting of who God created you to be. The question becomes are you going to agree with Him? By renewing our minds to God's Word, we learn His perfect will for our lives. The sooner you see who you are, the sooner you will learn what your role is in the Body of Christ.

The Power of I Am

Many people are not living up to who they truly are because of two little words they speak attached to negativity. People who say "I *am*" followed by a negative statement may be keeping themselves from their destiny. "I *am*" are two mighty words. We need to remember when God created the world—He spoke to it. He said let there be light, and there was. God only said what

He wanted to see! That means our words are powerful spiritual forces. If you want to achieve your destiny, you must understand the power in "I *am*."

"God replied to Moses, 'I am who I am. Say this to the people of Israel: I am has sent me to you'"
(Exodus 3:14, NLT).

If you have been saying phrases like, *"I am broke. I am so fat. I am so ugly. I am so stupid. I am in debt. I am never going to get my dreams."* Remember, life and death are in the power of the tongue, and those who love to talk will reap the consequences (Proverbs 18:21, NLT).

When you do this, you plant seeds of death and struggle in your life. But, do not fear because God and the spiritual power of your tongue can plant a new harvest.

Look, I have said a heck of a lot of death over my life too. Don't kick yourself. Instead, repent, asking for the Father to cancel all those words in Jesus' name. Then ask Him to help you plant prosperous seeds and to help you watch your tongue.

The fact is there will never be another you. Why not speak positive, amazing things about you? Some people mostly talk negative things about themselves. So, it's no surprise that they don't like themselves. Maybe you constantly say *I am* followed by a negative. If that's true, now's the time to change your ways!

One of the best ways to learn what you say is by having an accountability partner who calls you out every time you speak death. This may sound extreme, but it is amazing how your life can prosper from this one calibration.

When my husband and I were dating, I asked him to be my accountability partner, which helped him pay attention to his words. Anytime one of us spoke death, we gently called the other person out as agreed. We became very mindful that if we were going to speak death, to say nothing at all. Nowadays, the fruit of doing this has grown to where we refrain from watching entertainment shows that just put people or God down.

Remember, the less corrupt communication we let out of our mouth, the less corrupt things we will think and say about ourselves! Do you know a successful, joy-filled person who speaks death? Do you know anyone who speaks death who loves their life and is pleasant to be around? I don't! Those people are not necessarily dreadful to be around, but they aren't a walk in the park either. However, people who speak life, encouragement, and love tend to be more enjoyable to be around and are usually successful, content, and have tremendous joy. What do you have to lose?

Paul tells us in 2 Corinthians 4:18 we are not to look at the trouble we can see now but to fix our focus on things that cannot be seen. He continues by saying, it is the unseen things that are eternal. We cannot see the words we speak. Your words matter!

We are encouraged to speak or call things that are not as though they were (Romans 4:17). What does that mean? It means we are to call things as though they were not. God did this. He said what He wanted to see. He called light into existence, and it existed. Jesus did this, too, by casting out demons and healing people.

Where do you need to speak more life?

Prayer: Father God, help me to speak life and the words of Christ. Just as Jesus only spoke what you spoke, I would like to do the same. Father, please help me to get to know myself, as You know me. I want to be my authentic self, which I know is found in You only. Please help me to get to know myself and speak what I want to see. In Jesus' name, amen!

CHAPTER 18

Reframe It and Give It to God

Part of transforming your mindset into a victor means learning how to reframe the abuse, trauma, and negative experiences by identifying lessons you have learned and put the events into perspective. Believe it or not, every situation contains positive and negative components. Sometimes you may have to get the microscope out to identify the positives because they're so tiny. Other times, it takes actual time to pass before you can even identify the positive fruit in the situation. Nonetheless, it's still a positive. At some point, you need to choose to change the narrative in your mind about your past. The more oppressing you make it, the more oppressed you will be.

In your journal, do the following:

Create three columns

1. Label column #1 as "The event." Do not go into great detail about the event. Say enough to help you distinguish it from other painful events.
2. Label Column #2 "The Positives." Here, you will identify possible positive outcomes from the event. Think about what it has taught you about yourself.
3. Label Column #3 "How this can empower you." How does this information help you instead of hurting you?

It may sound like I am encouraging you to lie to yourself, but I am not. I am encouraging you to think more expansively and see more than you are allowing yourself to see. Life has many perspectives, and sometimes we can latch on to a narrative that is creating more harm than peace.

In Philippians, Paul writes, "And I want you to know, my dear brothers and sisters, that everything that has happened to me here has helped to spread the Good News" (Philippians 1:12, NLT).

When I first read this verse, a smile immediately appeared on my face. Paul is correct. There is the fortune of misfortune! Paul saw that his imprisonment allowed for the gospel to spread even further, which is why he was thankful for his misfortune. This is proof that God does overrule the wicked plans of the darkness of evil and brings triumph out of tragedy.

Yes, it also takes a person free from bitterness and the victim mindset to identify what the fortunes from the misfortune are. For years, I was bitter about my past. I was baffled, too unsure what was what. I knew deep down that my history was true, but I didn't want to believe it because there was so much I didn't understand. Then one day, as I was walking with the Lord to change my mentality, I decided to identify all the positives that resulted from my painful past. It was then that I, too, took on Paul's perspective. The fact of my reality is, I do not know if I would be where I am today had I not had the past I had. Today, after doing much healing and work with God, I am grateful I could go through what I went through if it means I can advance God's kingdom to some degree.

Due to my past, I am an extremely empathetic and very good listener. I have been told I am wise beyond my years. As a professional coach and soon-to-be licensed counselor, these are all necessary skills for me to have. I can relate to others on just about everything too. I humbly admit that it is rare for a client to share something with me that I have not personally gone through to some degree or another. Do you know how helpful this is when navigating a session?

I am also a very strong person, mentally, spiritually, and physically. It took me a while to see people telling me that I am strong as a compliment, but I would not be as strong today if I did not go through what I went through. The eating disorder taught me how to instill discipline, and that is still a lesson I leverage today but with a very different intent.

At some point, I chose to become more fearless with humans than fearful. I would tell myself, *"I have survived my brother. There is nothing another can do to me that he hasn't prepared me for."* I know how it sounds, but it is something that brought me comfort. Quite frankly, my thought process was, *I have survived my brother, so bring it on!* To clarify, that mentality was not meant to come off as arrogant but as an advocate for others. I know I have gone through more than the average person, and I was still mentally sane. Because of that, I would rather volunteer to endure more pain than to allow someone else to go through it. I knew I would be okay, and ironically, I always knew God was with me. I never wanted anyone to hurt the way I had hurt, so I was happy to advocate for another or take their place if it meant someone else escaped pain or trauma. There is nothing that someone else can do to me that my brother, at one level or another, hasn't prepared me to face.

Since I am mentally tough, I have remarkable resilience and focus. I know that I can achieve whatever

I put my mind to, and when I do it in alignment with the Father, I am genuinely unstoppable, just as you are! But, the greatest blessing of all is my past fueled me to seek a relationship with the Lord. When I saw that the Lord truly does take all the negative baggage from you and that living His way is the best mental health path you can choose, I became passionate about sharing the gospel with everyone and anyone. And that, my friend, is priceless! If me going through my past was for His benefit, then I will gladly do it again. As a child, I would ask God to redeem the pains of my past. In my heart, I knew He would, and He has!

God used everything and redeemed it! I have many strengths because of my past. However, I could not see them until I chose to break up with the victim mindset and open myself up to Him. If you give God your pain, He will give you your future! He will show you how that one painful event was the start of something incredible. But you must be willing to let it go, which is a process in itself.

Remember, hurting people hurt people.

When I took the time to identify all the positives that came from my abuse, I began to change my narrative. By changing the narrative, I began to see so much of my past and my family in different lights. I also decided to mindfully be curious about what drove my brother and mom to make their decisions. First off, I know my brother was exposed to some very serious witchcraft as a young toddler. We had a babysitter that did some cruel things to him, like once she locked my brother, who was two, in our creepy, copperhead-infested basement. Since my brother is older than me, I am unsure what else he went through before I arrived, but I know the things he did to me he was taught and wanted to take his anger out on me. The things he took his anger out on me for, I do understand. I would have preferred us to be friends, but I do get it. You see, our father was born in 1928! When I was out with my dad, people thought he was my grandfather as he had me when he was sixty-one! My father's age never bothered me, but it did my brother. He got picked on quite a lot for my dad's age, and the fact that he struggled with a severe case of dyslexia didn't help. When I add up the facts of my brother being upset about his father's age, being hazed for dyslexia, accompanied by the reality so much of our family died after my dad's death, I do get why he was so angry.

I am not condoning his behavior, but putting myself in his shoes, has helped me forgive him. I also know it was not really him, but the spirits he opened himself up to, which weren't always due to his choices. We all make mistakes. Yes, sometimes it is at the cost of another, but that is why we are to forgive, not condemn. If you aren't clear, I do love my brother, and we have a healthier relationship. The fact of the matter is we are different people that sometimes have to agree to disagree, but I would always help him out if he needed it. Love does cover a multitude of sins when you allow God's supernatural love to fill your heart. I encourage you to take some time today to identify all the positives that came about from your pain. When you have identified them, pray, asking God to redeem all that was stolen from you!

"The Lord is close to the brokenhearted;
he rescues those whose spirits are crushed"
(Psalm 34:18, NLT).

Leveraging Your Past

Do a quick mental rundown of your life up to this point. Quickly think about all the conflicts, difficulties, and struggles of your life. Great. Now, believe it or not—whether you see it or not—you have overcome them. Those events are all in the past, even if they happened thirty minutes ago.

Perhaps you did not overcome them in a victorious manner or in the way you desire to, but those adverse events are over. There may be some residue leftover, but at least they are over! The only conflict left from the past events is the one you choose to repeat in your head. Maybe you do not know how you move forward or how the battle ended, but it ended. That means everything will pass. Nothing can last forever but your soul and spirit. I hope this chapter gets you motivated about building your bridge to move from the life you have to your God-given life. You have to choose when you will break the ties with all that is hindering you, and only you can do that!

Start waking up every morning, thinking, *Today is going to be awesome because I'm doing life with Christ!*

Jesus makes it very clear He only speaks and does what His Father told Him to. Imagine if you allowed such dedication, focus, and commitment to the Father to be a part of your life. How many better and more educated choices would you make?

How do you do that? Well, first, you need to start seeing God as King in your life and not your pains, abusers, or whatever else is taking His spot! Then you start inviting Him into everything. Jesus remained in constant communication with the Father, and you can too. See God as your CEO! Check-in with Him regularly! Before you make a decision, ask God what He thinks about it. Remember to be open to hearing what God has to say! If you aren't sure if you heard Him, ask again. Sometimes, I ask God to provide me direction in a 1+1=2 type of way, so I can't miss it. We can live our lives just as Jesus exemplified here on earth. The only thing that is stopping you from doing so is you!

---

*"I tell you the truth, anyone who believes in me will do the
same works I have done, and even greater works, because I am
going to be with the Father"*
(John 14:12, NLT).

Would you please think of a struggle, conflict, or
negative experience that occurred that you have successfully moved forward from? It doesn't matter how
big or small it is. Perhaps it was when your manager
was bullying you or when a friend was bulldozing your
boundaries. Examine how you let this event go. I know
you might be thinking a harmless event compared to a
life-changing event is not the same. Here's the thing,
both people sinned, most likely, and wronged you. Do
you know God sees sin as sin, minus blasphemy of
the Holy Spirit? It is our human minds encouraged by
the devil who wants to make one wrong greater than
another.

What you want to identify is how did you move forward from something that was a negative experience?
What did you do, and what could you do better? Maybe
you find a decision you made consciously or unconsciously helped you move forward.

Nonetheless, you became committed to moving forward. When we identify what helped you let go and
move forward, we can copy and paste it to other situ-

ations. If you can do something well in one area, you can copy and paste it to another place. Yes, you might have to make some outfit changes, but those are details! We know life is about our mindset, thoughts, what we say, and our focus. What are you saying about that narrative that is constantly replaying in your mind? What would happen if you changed that narrative to a more life-giving one?

Prayer: Father, please help me see the positives and blessings in the painful experiences I am having a hard time letting go of. Help me recall how I moved past certain negative situations too. I ask that You bring to light all that I am holding on to that is stealing from me. Help me to surrender it to you. Help me to see the fortunes from my misfortunes. As You take it from me, help me to see it as You do. In Jesus' name, amen.

CHAPTER 19

Resilience

What you might not notice is that event you chose to move forward from took resilience. Ironically, while life is going to have troubles and moments of pain, resilience is not something we are naturally born with, but we must work to develop and instill. How does one build or increase their resilience? We will examine that and talk about implementing mental resilience to help you continuously strengthen the skill.

What Is Resilience?

The definition originates from the Latin verb *resilire*, which means "to leap" or "rebound," and the Oxford Dictionary of English as "being able to withstand or recover quickly from difficult conditions."[25] I think we can do better than resilience and be an *overcomer*! To be an overcomer, you need a strong foundation and capability of mental resilience. I think overcoming is more enticing because who wants to bounce back? I do not know

25 Young, 2014.

about you, but I wish to overcome. To me, overcoming is about bouncing back and moving forward all in one swift motion. I want to be better than I was before the adversity. Who doesn't want that?

Perhaps this illustration will help. Imagine yourself driving on the highway. As you continue moving along the route, you approach a car in front of you that is cruising at a slightly slower speed. Not wanting to be slowed down, you contemplate changing lanes, but there is a car next to you that is about to match your pace. You can either do nothing, change lanes, staying parallel to where you are, or accelerating forward while changing lanes. An example of resilience would be changing lanes and staying parallel to where you were. Whereas an example of overcoming would be changing lanes while simultaneously accelerating forward.

Psychologically speaking, all resilience means is to have the ability to tolerate psychological discomfort.

Resiliency is about effectively and healthily coping with negative feelings that arise from negative experiences while still functioning in one's daily life. It also includes recognizing and having the awareness to take time off from everyday responsibilities in the face of extreme stress like a death of a loved one or divorce.

Let me clarify this one thing that many forget. Responding with resilience does not mean you are not feeling pain, discomfort, or negative emotions. An example of practicing resilience would be acknowledging that the situation is one situation, not your entire life, and then identifying what is in your control and doing something about it. Take note that leveraging acceptance is part of moving towards resilience. Also, notice how thinking traps like catastrophizing can prevent an individual from practicing resilience.

Essentially, we are talking about a concept we have already covered—*"This, too, shall pass."*

Many of the most stressed individuals add to their suffering by wasting time and bandwidth by not taking their thoughts captive but instead meditating on worry or things out of their control. Since maintaining a resilient focus relies on your thoughts, we will go through how you take your thoughts captive and why taking your thoughts captive is so liberating. There is no benefit to worry or harbor on thoughts that are out of control. We must learn to have the discipline to focus and do what we can about a situation and then let the rest go. Besides, the sooner you give the situation to God, the sooner His will can be done about the matter!

From experience, it is one thousand times easier to let something go when you trust God with it. Not letting go will hinder a person's ability to respond with resilience because not letting go causes one to forgo the reality change is always happening. The Greek philosopher of the late 6th century, Heraclitus, said, "No man ever steps in the same river twice, for it's not the same river, and he's not the same man."

Think about what he is saying for a moment. You cannot step in a river and hit the same molecules twice, even if you step in the same spot. That spot has changed even if you don't see it. Such truth is the same for man. Just at a biological level, we are always constantly changing. Cells are dying and being recreated. We are continually evolving both mentally, physically, and spiritually. Growth happens, and we don't always see it.

Resiliency, as mentioned earlier, is not innate but develops over time. If you are getting frustrated that you are not mentally tough enough in situations, give yourself some grace. Like many things, it takes time to develop, but you can develop it.

Developing Resilience

How does one develop resilience? How do you not allow adversity to overtake you and cause your emotions to control you? There are few ways to do this. I will tell you the number one thing that helped me grow my resilience was allowing God into everything, remembering I do everything for Him, changing my self-talk, and leveraging hindsight. I encourage you to journal about life. It is one of the best ways to strengthen self-awareness and learn from your mistakes. I will quickly go through a list of ways to develop and build resilience, but they are not in any particular order. What might work for you might not work for me and vice versa. That is okay. We are all unique, one-of-a-kind beings. Celebrate you by focusing on what works for you. This is your life and no one else's. Don't worry about what Jane is doing—focus on your growth.

Learn how to accept what has happened and that you cannot change it. There is that word again: accept! Acceptance is a powerful mental skill. The same way we learned how to practice self-acceptance is like accepting situations and external realities. You want to identify what can be learned from past mistakes, failures, and emotional outbursts. Replay those events objectively and invite God in. Ask for His wisdom about the situation. He will give it to you. What could you have done better? How will you do it next time? Yes, there will most likely be a next time, so preparing yourself and visualizing how you will handle the unpleasant event next time is powerful!

Give yourself a purpose and develop a game plan. Goals are hugely important to a healthy mindset. Get clear on how you want to act. If you don't like how discomfort stops you, talk to the Father about it and identify what you wish you would do in those moments.

For instance, some people hate to hear criticism. One critical thing that causes them to lash out. They act as if you killed their firstborn. Instead of lashing out, change your self-talk when someone says something critical. You can choose to see it as attacking you or helping you, or even as someone's opinion. Just because a human said it does not mean it's true. I know that for me, when I would have to hear constructive criticism, I mentally prepared myself. I would tell myself, *"It's okay. They are just trying to help you. See it from their point of view, then pray to God about whether it's true or not."*

Additionally, I quickly learned that if I was offended, there was some truth to what was being said. I could either get upset and pout or do something about it. I hope you are noticing a victim allows information to stop them; victors allow information to help them. One is passive, and the other is proactive.

We want to find reasons to stay motivated not to participate in unhealthy behavior. I do not know about you, but I would bet you that when you allow your emotions to control you and react hysterically, you become drained. Fighting is draining and time-consuming. It often leaves us feeling worse than we did before. I have never met anyone who was spiritually rejuvenated and empowered after an at-your-throat-type of a fight. Find your own strategies that will take you from where you are to where you will be, which will take experimenting. When you choose to experiment, you can learn so much about yourself. It's important to remember to refrain from trying to get it "right" because you are experimenting, which means you may have a few failed attempts. That's okay. Change the hypothesis and keep going!

Get the facts! What has made this difficulty occur, and what can you do about them? Do what you can and move forward! Choose not to look back. Again, focus on what is in your control and move forward. Again, ask the Father to help you discern this!

Put it in perspective. The best way to do this is, again, to remain objective. You got to see the event without your emotions fueling you. What may be going on in the other person's life for them to respond this way? We are not working to justify their behavior but to identify what may be fueling it. It's applying a curious, eagle-eye out look to the situation at hand.

Another compelling question you can ask yourself is, what is the worst-case scenario? Is it losing a friend, a loved one, or death? Whatever it may be, choose to obtain the belief that no matter what, you will be okay! Again, this is where I encourage leaning on the Father. I always remind myself that God has me, and He will not abandon me. I'm good. I'm great. I'm protected. I've got God, and He blesses me.

Time and Patience

This one is a little more challenging for me, but hopefully, it is not for you. Time is your friend, not your enemy. What I have learned over the years and through my adversity is many things work themselves out if you give the person or the situation time. If you can develop the patience to be okay in the unknown or be okay with not being okay, many amazing things can come out of the pain. Remember, God is outside of time.

But, what about building on your resilience. Is there a different way to do that? No, not really. If you want to build your resilience besides using the above techniques, you must commit to not giving up mentally. Times might be hard. As a human, you will fail, but that does not mean you quit or stop trying to succeed.

Do you know what Proverbs says about failure?

"The godly may trip seven times, but they will get up again. But one disaster is enough to overthrow the wicked" (Proverbs 24:16, NLT).

For most people, one difficult conversation or hardship will cause them to abandon the ship. Essentially one thing defeats them. Yet, the Bible says we will face areas of disaster where our perseverance is necessary. The Bible also says that when a righteous man falls into trouble or disaster, he will recover each time. However, the wicked will stumble into ruin from a single misfortune.

Understand that God has made provision for you to fail! Also, understand that if someone is not allowing you to fail, you must plead failure. We all fail. Since God made provision for failure, you should recognize the truth that you may fail a handful of times, but it's the righteous man who gets back up!

Another awesome thing you can do every day to help you have better resilience is to practice problem-solving. Yes, that is right play problem-solving games like word puzzles or games that require you to strategize. Part of resilience is learning how to try a handful of angles and not giving up! Another thing you can do is leverage your strengths. You are innately great at something. Whatever that something is, and deep down, you know what it is, you might be hesitant about it, and that's okay, leverage it.

I am great at finding solutions. I am also great at encouraging others—so why not encourage myself in moments of adversity?

The last way of building resilience focuses on leveraging past success. But, if you feel you have never bounced back from any trouble or are struggling to bounce back from the adversity still affecting you, I want you to find someone else who has overcome a similar hardship. I want you to research their life and read about how they overcome that trauma and then emulate it. I think we overlook the power of emulation. Jesus is a great place to start!

As someone who is kinesthetic, I love to watch people. Emulation is how I have learned how to do so much.

For instance, in my early twenties, I wanted to be more loving, but I didn't know how. Love was foreign to me. Yet, I had this spiritual mother in my life who is the definition of love and acceptance. I have never felt judged by her, and I am so comfortable with her! One day, I asked her what made her so loving. Of course, she said Jesus. So I started pursuing Jesus in a different avenue. I also did other things that she did, like leverage empathy, understanding, and grace. Another example is when I was in undergrad at art school. I had to take two drawing classes, and at the time, I was not a skilled drawer. However, mind over matter, right? Especially when it's God's will for you. I watched how my instructor held his pencil and moved his wrist. Essentially, I did my best to break down his fundamentals, and then I copied them. You can do what you believe you can or cannot do!

Foundation of Resilience

Resilient people who succeed at practicing resilience in adversity know there is hope amid setbacks and difficulties. They believe that life will get better. They do not allow an event or misfortune to control the rest of their life. Instead, they choose to focus on a joy-filled life, positivity, and Jesus. Understand that just because you face adversity does not mean you have to agree with negativity. It is about adapting and responding with positivity, not the woe is me phenomenon. One way you could refer to a resiliently strong individual is by saying they are a tough-minded optimist. Norman Vincent Peale defines tough-minded optimists as a determined, focused, solution-oriented kind of personality. A person who keeps moving forward no matter what anybody says, does, doesn't do, as long as they know what they are doing is right, ethical, and worthy.[26] I want to add to his definition. A tough-minded optimist, a resilient person, does what the Lord tells them no matter how much fear tries to hold them back. Start to see resilience as another form of obedience to the Father. Don't let anyone or anything keep you from doing what God wants you to do in your life!

How does one develop such a mindset of tough but optimistic?

First and foremost, like most of what we are discussing here—it's a choice! You have to decide and believe you can do this. The reality is you need to stop letting external things bring you peace and positivity and allow the Lord to be your joy and strength.

"This is a sacred day before our Lord. Don't be dejected and sad, for the joy of the LORD is your strength!"
(Nehemiah 8:10b, NLT)

---

26 Peale, 1961.

If you do not believe you can do this, you will not become a tough-minded optimist. Secondly, it's your self-talk or lack thereof. Your self-talk *must* be disciplined, encouraging, and focused. The bottom line is if God's not going to talk that way to you, why are you? If you are not going to talk that way to a friend, why are you doing it to yourself?

I encourage you to find self-talk that encourages you and motivates you in moments where you may not want to hear what the other person has to say.

The third thing you must develop is faith in God. You must grow your faith and suffocate your fear, which can only be conquered through Christ! If you haven't come to terms with God being in every part of your life, do so! Get to the point where you only want to do what He wants you to do. We can't severe our flesh and Him. You must pick one! You must start putting into practice that God is for you, not against you. For some, trusting God in your life might be complex or a foreign idea.

I was raised in a part-time Methodist home. Meaning we only participated in our faith on Sundays for an hour or two. We did not talk about God any other time but in the walls of the church. I was born with a spiritual gift and desire of always praying and talking to God, but I did not *really* know God, if you get what I mean. For most of my life, I did live my way. Trusting first and foremost in myself and then God. Around twenty-five years of age, I got to experience the trip of a lifetime. I went to South Africa, where I was working on a wildlife documentary. In Africa, I met a man who helped me understand God's importance, power, and love. At that time, I couldn't fathom God's love for me entirely, but once I surrendered my life to Him, awesome things began to happen. I finally discovered my purpose and what I wanted to live for. I would encourage you to open yourself up to God. Take baby steps. He won't rush you. He meets you!

The entirety of this book will help you build resilience. Resourcefulness, perseverance, self-confidence, self-discipline, level-headedness, mental flexibility, positive thinking, positive relationships, problem-solving, and healthy coping skills are the blueprints to resiliency. You can do this! When you expand positive thinking to optimism—always believing the future holds something excellent for you, there is no way you will not bounce back and move forward.

> *"'For I know the plans I have for you,' says the LORD.*
> *'They are plans for good and not for disaster, to give*
> *you a future and a hope'"*
> (Jeremiah 29:11, NLT).

Here is a *powerful* affirmation I want you to all start saying and believing about yourself.

God made me strong. I see myself as I am—strong. With God's help, I am not weak! I am strong! I have what it takes! I will do all the things that are in my God-given will. Thank You, God, for my strength. Thank You for giving me a mighty and good future. Thank You for showing me how to operate out of the mind of Christ! Thank You for Your everlasting, unconditional love.

Believe you can, and you will! If life is extra hard for you, I encourage you to have a real honest talk with yourself, where God is the mediator. The fact of the matter is you just might be making your life harder for you than you need to.

Cultivating your potential inner tough-minded self takes time. If you are weak, you are spending more time seeing, visualizing in your mind, and practicing being weak. It is the same with anger, depression, or any other negative sensation. It's even true for those who are chronically sick. You become what you think!

Prayer: Father, help me to be persistent, focused, and resilient like Jesus. I know in times where I feel afraid or uncomfortable, I want to quit. I know this is most likely my flesh. Please help me to crucify it so I can do Your will in my life. Father, please use me how You best see fit. Father, I know there are times where I plan my own way and exclude You. Please help me to stop doing that. Please help me only to do what You want me to do! Thank You for Your grace, love, Son, and using me in Your kingdom. In Jesus' name, amen.

CHAPTER 20

Taking Thoughts Captive

Have you ever realized your power?

God created you in His image, which means you have two types of power. He gave you incredible authority through Christ and the power of free will. These powers are so potent that they run into our thoughts. We can think about whatever we want to think about, which means we can control our thinking. We can direct our thoughts on amazing things. Most of our thoughts are generated by the outside world. What we see around us externally will trigger our ideas many times. I believe some of that *external stimulus* is, sometimes, a spirit flying over my head. Think about it. How many times have you been driving thinking about how much you loved your dog, only to start killing off your family and preparing to survive a zombie apocalypse? In these situations, there were no external stimuli, per se, that you saw with your eyes that caused you to go down that route.

Whereas other times, perhaps you have been in a conversation with a friend and saw something triggering you to think about something super random. Since sometimes our thoughts are created by the outside world, whether by suggestion or what may come across as absolute fact, what is more alarming is how someone can impulsively accept such offers without ever challenging or researching the accuracy of what is presented. Many blindly receive thoughts from the outside world without cross-examination if the idea is accurate or aligning with your beliefs, let alone the Bible.

We tend to question such external suggested thoughts after agreeing with the thought, making it a part of our belief hierarchy, only to hear another person's opinion conflict with it or to have an experience that conflicts with the belief. This is the reality of Fear of rejection. We blindly accept anyone's opinion with no regard for the truth. This mentality can also put us on the path of confusion and doubt when we realize the suggestion doesn't work. Do you see how sneaky the devil can be? Remember, he is the author of confusion! The American poet, Ella Wheeler Wilcox, was once quoted, saying,

Man is what he thinks. Not what he says,
reads, or hears. By persistent thinking you
can undo any condition which exists. You can
free yourself from any chains, whether poverty, sin, ill health, unhappiness or Fear.
Ella Wheeler Wilcox
(All grammar and spelling has been left
unedited.)

I couldn't agree more. The Bible also speaks to this.
The mind controls the brain; the brain does not control the mind. How is your mind controlling your brain?
Are you focusing on being sick? What are you telling
your brain to produce inside of you? Understand that
your thoughts will become your words; your words will
become your action; your actions will become your habits; and your habits will become a character, which ultimately becomes your future.

I know all this to be true because I once had a terrible mindset. My victim mindset produced bad fruit
in my life. I didn't think about being self-less or obedient to God, so I wasn't. I was on the fast track to hell.
I may have acknowledged and accepted Christ, but I
was not living for Him nor was I seeking a relationship
with Him. How can you be obedient to someone when
you don't know what they are asking you to do? I am so
grateful that the Father kept calling me to Him, and I

am so happy I answered. I always wanted a deeper relationship with Christ, but I had no idea how to do that!

Let's say you are depressed, and you talk to your friend about how you are depressed in a complaining manner where you don't want to change or do anything about it but focus on being depressed. Do you know what you are doing? You are feeding thoughts of depression. What happens? Your depression worsens, you become anxious, and change seems forever away—if not impossible. This is one of the main reasons why talk therapy does not work. In fact, after World War II, the focus of therapy shifted from what was going right in one's life to hyper-focusing on all that was going wrong in one's life.[27]

When you constantly talk about your problems in a problem-centered manner, you strengthen the synaptic nerve connections, enforcing them to become your dominant way of thinking. So, stop talking about the issue. Start talking about the solutions. Perhaps this is why God wants us to be content and thankful in everything because He knows the cost?

I am not encouraging you not to be curious about your thoughts. I am merely alerting you to get clear on your agenda. Are you saying what you are saying to find solutions, have someone rescue you, vent, or complain? Now, yes, learning these insights may take doing

---

27 Peterson, 2006.

it and reflecting even to understand your intent. That's okay. Learning is one thing. Passively doing nothing is another.

Proverbs 29:11 even attests that a foolish person vents all their feelings, whereas the wise hold their feelings back. Meaning a fool uncontrollably, without restraint or consideration, pours out their anger. However, wise people will restrain themselves until they can clearly articulate their frustration. Their intention for expressing their frustration focuses on resolving it or communicating it to get another objective perspective. Ultimately, they are trying to get unstuck and are willing to do the work, whereas fool wants to perform lip service.

Yes, you might feel depressed, but we know feelings lie and change quite quickly. Focus on solutions. As a believer, depression is a great indicator you are not thinking on Philippians 4:8 but are thinking self-righteously. What can you do to bring yourself in the present moment, grateful and appreciative for life? Start getting curious. Review the things you have been meditating on. Even ask yourself, *Who told me I was depressed?* Who told you what you are feeling is whatever it is? Who told you, you were sick? Who told you, you were unhappy? Who told you to kill yourself? Stop blindly accepting the sensations of the body and retrace that thought with your spiritual eyes!

When I fell into depression, I knew it is because my thoughts have shifted off God and on to fear accompanied with a *woe is me* thought process. You know, poor me because I don't have whatever it was that I thought would empower me to be happy. It's the *if only* thinking trap. Or it's the Spirit of Fear taking over me, and I am allowing myself to respond negatively with disappointment about what I don't want to see happen when in reality, it hasn't happened yet. It's amazing how much taking your eyes off Jesus can deteriorate your quality of life. Pay attention to what you are thinking about and where your focus is!

When you focus on negative words and thoughts, research suggests you can begin to damage your brain's key structures that regulate memory, feelings, and emotions. *Yikes!* Get this, when you vocalize negativity, you are only adding stress into your world. Part of adopting the victor mindset is identifying where you are making life harder on yourself, which, in turn, can affect others. If you speak negativity, you are doing just that. Speaking negativity causes stress chemicals to release in your brain and the brain of the listener.[28]

You see, our brain only knows what we tell it. If you tell your brain you are unsafe, your brain will respond. If you tell your brain you are safe, your brain will respond to that too. Your brain doesn't know the differ-

---

28 Newberg & Waldman, 2013.

ence between the past, present, and future either. Your brain also doesn't understand sarcasm and joking. You will still have a response to it. Think about this for a second when you watch a scary or violent movie or even a happy movie, you have a physiological reaction to what you are seeing, don't you? Even though you are safely in your home when you watch the character run for its life, you are not sitting there telling your brain you are safe. You probably aren't even thinking about that either. Instead, you are yelling at the TV screen, *"Run, run."* And you are doing it in a manner that causes you to get stressed because everything you are seeing and telling yourself is causing your brain to make your body react with adrenaline. Start paying attention to what you are watching. How can God help deliver you from the Spirit of Fear if you are going to keep opening your eyes to it? Stop being curious about evil!

Why does your brain do that? Well, there is something in your brain called the thalamus. It is in the center of your brain, and it kind of looks like a walnut. Your thalamus relates sensory information about the outside world to other parts of our brains. When we imagine or even see something on the tv screen, the data is sent to the thalamus. Your thalamus treats thoughts and fantasies the same way through processing them with your five senses. It cannot distinguish between inner and external realities.[29] This is why when you think you are safe, your brain responds, or when you believe you are unsafe, your brain responds with worry and presumes there is a real threat at hand. What you think is one of the most important things you need to be aware of. God makes it clear that we are not to let His word depart from our eyes or lips. I believe He tells us this so we can have more life.

The Foundation of Thought Control

I want you to rate yourself on how well you practice controlling your thoughts. One is the worst, and ten is the best. What would you put yourself at?

Before I learned how to do this, mine was a one!

How often do you think like Jesus? Would you say your thoughts are in alignment with what and how Jesus thought? Or would you be a bit embarrassed if you had to discuss some of your thoughts with Jesus?

No, you cannot control what enters your mind, but you can choose what thoughts you participate with, agree with, or meditate on!

Since you cannot control what enters your mind, you can choose what you come into agreement with. Here is where we must pay careful attention too. It can be easy to play something out in your mind's imagination, only for you to realize that you just killed off your family. You

---

29 Newberg & Waldman, 2013.

can unintentionally agree with the spirits of darkness through thought.

"Can two people walk together
without agreeing on the direction?"
(Amos 3:3, NLT)

I believe our brain responds to spiritual components because the Bible tells us they do! We can agree with demonic forces, principalities of darkness—by agreeing with specific thoughts. Please remember that the only way the enemy can get inside of you is by you coming into agreement with them through buying their lies. When you buy their lies, you have given them authority over you, which means you have traded in Jesus' authority for that of the devil!

Principalities of darkness have no authority unless you give them authority! Please don't give it to them!

And [I pray] that the eyes of your heart [the very center
and core of your being] may be enlightened [flooded
with light by the Holy Spirit], so that you will know and
cherish the hope [the divine guarantee, the confident
expectation] to which He has called you, the riches of His
glorious inheritance in the saints (God's people), and [so
that you will begin to know] what the immeasurable and
unlimited and surpassing greatness of His [active, spiri-

tual] power is in us who believe. These are in accordance with the working of His mighty strength which He produced in Christ when He raised Him from the dead and seated Him at His own right hand in the heavenly places, far above all rule and authority and power and dominion [whether angelic or human], and [far above] every name that is named [above every title that can be conferred], not only in this age and world but also in the one to come. And He put all things [in every realm] in subjection under Christ's feet, and appointed Him as [supreme and authoritative] head over all things in the church, which is His body, the fullness of Him who fills and completes all things in all [believers].

Ephesians 1:18-23 (AMP)

Whatever lies might enter your mind when you think about something, be careful because you could be letting something evil in. That is why Paul tells us to bring the thought into the obedience of Christ. You speak the truth to that thought!

Perhaps hearing the phrase "think like Jesus" intimidates you. Maybe you are thinking like Jesus will cut out all the fun, but you're mistaken.

I've had the *time my life with Jesus!* I've had more fun with Jesus being a part of my life than when He was a distant cousin. Before Jesus was the center of my life, I was suffering! I was hurting. I was asking man to do what God only could do for me. I am so thankful that you become a new creation when you come into Christ because I don't remember that old self. Praise the Lord.

If you want to ride the rollercoaster of your life—Jesus is going to give it to you! It's going to be the most fulfilling and satisfying ride of your life. The ride is better than you can even *imagine!* Yeah, there's going to be bumps, drops, and excitement. A roller coaster going straight is boring, and a rollercoaster where you are blindfolded and have no idea what is going on is terrifying. *But* when you take that rollercoaster ride with Jesus, *victory* is always at the end! Doing things Jesus' way is the best way!

We know we're either speaking death or life (Proverbs 18:21). Just like you're either filled with God or filled with the devil. If you are filled with God, you will have and therefore do *godly things*, just as you will do the opposite if you are filled with evil.

We learn this in 1 John 3:9-10:

> Those who have been born into God's family
> do not make a practice of sinning because
> God's life is in them. So they can't keep on
> sinning because they are children of God. So
> now we can tell who are children of God and
> who are children of the devil. Anyone who

does not live righteously and does not love
other believers does not belong to God.

1 John 3:9-10 (NLT)

Since Jesus was both man and God, we then know
Jesus only had godly thoughts.

I believe, since Jesus was successful at having holy
thoughts and keeping His mind focused on His Father's
kingdom, then we can too. But first, we're going to have
to renew our minds. We will have to learn how to think
like Jesus so we can operate in the mind of Christ (1 Corinthians 2:16). To think like Jesus, we must spend time
with Jesus, which comes through reading the Word. It's
hard to think like anyone when you don't know them.

If you are a child of God—if you've accepted Jesus
Christ as your Lord and Savior—and if you have the
mind of Christ as Paul says in Corinthians, then your
thoughts—your thinking needs to be an alignment with
Jesus. *No ifs, ands, or buts!*

---

*"For I have not spoken on My own authority; but
the Father who sent Me gave Me a command, what
I should say and what I should speak"*
(John 12:49, NKJV).

Jesus has taught you not the things of men but the
profound, everlasting truths of God.

In all of Jesus' private conversations with His disciples or others, He, as man, commanded and spoke through the constant inspiration of the Holy Spirit. He never had His own agenda but of that which His Father instructed Him to do.

Jesus's doctrine was not human but divine. He only spoke what His Father told Him. For Him to only speak what the Father said to Him means Jesus's heart was filled with love for His Father.

"For where your treasure is, there your heart will be also"
(Matthew 6:21, NIV).

Jesus's treasure was living obedient to His Father's will—to please His Father. Jesus was only afraid of being separated from His Father—we see that right before He goes to the cross. Learning how to take your thoughts captive is wanting to get to know and live by the Father's will like Jesus did! It's having that deep desire and conviction to want to live for Him. This conviction empowers you to pay more attention to your thoughts, stopping you from blindly accepting everything that enters your mind. You turn from believing your mind to being mindfully curious about your thoughts and running them all through the filter of the Bible.

"For out of the abundance of the heart the mouth speaks" (Matthew 12:34b, NKJV).

Speech is the picture of the mind. Jesus's mind was filled with the heavens. He thought spiritually, not worldly, and that is what we must train our minds to do as disciples of Christ.

To think spiritually!

For though we walk in the flesh, we do not war according to the flesh. For the weapons of our warfare are not carnal but mighty in God for pulling down strongholds, casting down arguments and every high thing that exalts itself against the knowledge of God, bringing every thought into captivity to the obedience of Christ, and being ready to punish all disobedience when your obedience is fulfilled.

2 Corinthians 10:3-6 (NKJV)

The battle in our mind is spiritual.

The Spirit of Fear wants you to catastrophize "what if" yourself and should yourself to death, as well as any other thinking trap. Spirits of darkness will stop you from focusing on faith and God's promises for your life. The devil wants you to agree with him and make you feel as if hope and God's love for you do not exist. The enemy wants you to believe nothing good is going to come. But it's lies! He's selling you lies.

He wants you to use your imagination to project into the future *what you do not want to happen*, which is Fear. The devil doesn't want you to project faith-filled thoughts into the future! Why?

The more you think about something, the more it becomes a part of you.

What are your dominant thoughts?

What has your thinking created?

The Mental Waiting Room

Paul tells us to take every thought captive. He doesn't say some thoughts; he doesn't say one a day—he says all thoughts. The best description I can give you for taking your thoughts captive is to keep them in a waiting room, like at a doctor's office. Imagine if you didn't check in with the receptionist and just went back and saw the doctor? The receptionist would stop you! We must do the same with our thoughts. Before you agree to partner with a thought, make sure it's on the patient log. The only thoughts that qualify to be on the patient log are thoughts that are obedient to Christ. If the thought is not obedient, make it obedient or tell it to go!

You have to make all your thoughts obedient to Christ. Not only are you to take each thought captive—to put each thought in a mental waiting room before it can spend time with you—but to make that thought obedient to Christ.

How many thoughts do you think the average person has in a day? The average person has more than six thousand thoughts a day, and my research said it could be up to seventy thousand thoughts a day. Of those thoughts, 80 percent were negative, and 95 percent of them were the same repetitive thoughts—and we learn from repetition! That means you may have to take seventy thousand thoughts captive a day.

Wow, I hope you have Jesus's yoke on your neck because you will be exhausted. We know in neuroscience, when we're rewiring our brain, we're going to face resistance, and it will take additional energy. Our brains are not going to want to go there at first, and that is why I believe God tells us not to do life without Him because we need His strength in everything! We need the Godhead to help us transform our thinking. Self-will won't do it!

We need the Father's wisdom, Jesus's strength, and the Holy Spirit's guidance to take thoughts captive.

Since we think about the same thing repeatedly, the sooner you meditate on scripture all day and night, the sooner you will control your thinking. Some people need to stop lying to themselves. The truth is you know when a thought is obedient to Christ or not, and if you don't, well, great! Now, you know you need to read your

Bible more! See another win-win, as Paul reminds us. You can't lose when walking with Christ!

What do you do when you are holding a thought in your mental waiting room? You will not let it out of the holding room until you make sure it is obedient to God, and if it's not, what do you do with it?

1. Cast the thought down.

Paul tells us to take all thoughts and imaginations and anything that exalts itself against the Father and bring it into obedience. I see this as taking wallpaper down. You are stripping that thought of all its power, exposing the lies, and speaking the truth over it.

2. Tell the thought to be quiet!

Now, there may be times where that thought is a talker. Some are sneaky. So when this happens, tell it to shut up! Let the thought know it has no power or authority over you! "'Be quiet!' Jesus said sternly. 'Come out of him!' Then the demon threw the man down before them all and came out without injuring him" (Luke 4:35, NLT).

3. Command the thought to go!

Once you have brought God's light onto that thought, use your authority in Christ. Command the thought to go now in the name of Jesus. Break authority with it.

Command it never to enter you again. You have authority in Christ! Use it!

> When Jesus saw that the crowd of onlookers was
> growing, he rebuked the evil spirit. "Listen, you
> spirit that makes this boy unable to hear and
> speak," he said. "I command you to come out of
> this child and never enter him again!"
>
> Mark 9:25 (NLT)

4. Use the Word of God.

If all else fails, keep saying the Word of God. Speak the truth to yourself because the truth is eternal. God's Word is eternal. "Put on salvation as your helmet, and take the sword of the Spirit, which is the Word of God" (Ephesians 6:17, NLT).

You tell that thought to go now in the name of Jesus! You say I am not participating with you. Then, direct your attention to something representing love, like a favorite memory, a favorite Bible scripture, or praise the Father.

The reality is sometimes you are going to need to distract yourself. Spiritual warfare is what we are talking about here, and it can be tiring. However, if you tell yourself, "I'm not going to think about that," you most likely will. For instance, if I say don't think about a white elephant, I know your mind goes there. Not thinking about not thinking never works!

It's a functional distraction in psychology, but in this case, it's how we submit our minds back to God.

In my practice, I encourage my clients to do the love memory exercise. I tell my clients to be prepared for the enemy's attacks—for rumination—negative thinking—by having a list of their favorite love memories ready to go because your brain is easily deceived. Remember, love is very powerful. When you think about a love memory, your brain releases oxytocin, and that oxytocin can break the negative thinking. Your brain does not know the difference between the past, present, or future. Your brain is easily tricked.

Since your brain thinks about repetition, the more you think about holy things, the love you have in your life, and why your life is going right, the sooner you will keep yourself focused on the things above.

If every good and perfect gift is from above, why would you lease your mental real estate to the devil? Some people spend more time glorifying the devil than the Father. Renew your mind—retrain your mind to think like Jesus. Understand you have to set out to do this consciously. It will not happen by accident.

I believe one of the only ways to prevent your thinking—your thoughts from coming into agreement with the devil is by following what Joshua 1:8 (NLT) states,

"Study this Book of Instruction continually. Meditate on it day and night so you will be sure to obey everything written in it. Only then will you prosper and succeed in all you do."

This world will tempt you. That is a guarantee. The enemy will tempt you, and it's easy to be fooled, especially when you're playing on both teams. Some of us want to be a part of God's kingdom and want to do many things the world does that God disagrees with. Praise the Lord! He still loves us, even when we are disobedient, telling Him we know what's best. Oh, I hope you see the foolishness in that. However, part of this victory is getting clear on which team you are going to play for and sticking to that team! Please pick team Jesus!

Resisting Temptation

Temptation is coming, and the enemy is looking for who he can devour! Will you be one of them?

James 4:7 makes it very clear, and people miss this. They think, "Oh, I'll just resist the devil, and he's going to go," but that's not what it says!

"Therefore submit to God.
Resist the devil and he will flee from you"
(James 4:7, NKJV).

James says, *first submit yourself to God!* So what are you supposed to do first? Submit yourself to God! What does that mean; what does submitting yourself to God mean?

It means to obey God!

Get clear on whose side you're on. Whose team are you on? God's or the devil?

We remind the devil and ourselves that we are disciples of God, not followers of the enemy. Remember, you are a subordinate to God!

When you look throughout scripture, and Jesus is talking to anything demonic, He takes authority over it. When the devil tempted Jesus, do you know what Jesus said?

"But Jesus told him, 'No! The Scriptures say, 'People do not live by bread alone, but by every word that comes from the mouth of God'" (Matthew 4:4, NLT).

Guess what? The devil kept tempting Him, which means he will do the same to you too. He, too, can be persistent. So, Jesus responded again!

"Jesus responded, 'The Scriptures also say, 'You must not test the Lord your God'" (Matthew 4:7, NLT).

The devil *still* didn't quit. What does Jesus finally say?

"Get out of here, Satan," Jesus told him. "For the Scriptures say, 'You must worship the Lord your

God and serve only him. Then the devil went
away, and angels came and took care of Jesus.'"

Matthew 4:10-11 (NLT)

When Jesus was tempted, He spoke scripture—He
reminded the devil who's the real boss, and in time the
enemy left Him!

My point is—*say scripture!* Take the time to identify
some verses you can say to get the devil off you! Reciting scripture is how you take your mind off the enemy's
potentially enticing invitation to sin. He wants you to
accept it, and repeating God's Word is how you tell him
you have rejected his invitation. Get your mind back on
God! Start thinking about the things above!

You meditate all day and night regardless of if you're
aware of it or not. You're always thinking about something even when you aren't even aware of it, and that is
why you are to bury God's Word in your hearts.

"I will meditate on Your precepts,
And contemplate Your ways"
(Psalm 119:15, NKJV).

As disciples, we are never to let God's Word depart
from our eyes but to meditate on it day and night! This
is one way you can practice thought control because renewing your mind is complex and the only and fastest

way to do it is by reciting scripture! Choose to speak life, which is found in scripture!

Believers are in a war—spiritual warfare. Prepare for the battle because it's coming. Find your scripture so you can start speaking to the lies that the enemy is selling.

Prayer: Father God, Thank You for Your Word and Your Son. Thank You for giving me eternal life. I need help taking my thoughts captive as Your Word encourages. Please help me to discern, learn, and successfully take my thoughts captive. Help me renew my mind to Your Word and help me do life Your way and not my way. Thank You for building me up and showing me how to live for You in everything I do. In Jesus' name, amen.

CHAPTER 21

Armorning Up

Not that we have clarified what a victim mindset looks like and clarified what you need to do with the help of the Lord to renew your mind and start seeing yourself as a victor. Let's focus on ways you can remain in the victor mindset, regardless of what is occurring in your external or internal world.

How do you remain in this mindset? Practice, but by also keeping in constant communication with the Father. Keep doing it regardless of how well you think you are doing. Keep praying to God and keep relying on His strength. However, you must learn how to put on the mental armor, known as God's armor, to protect your victor mindset from turning back into a victim mindset. This is not Cinderella. No one is turning back into a pumpkin. The best metaphor I can think of to describe the importance of protecting your victor mindset is to think back to medieval times, where people were working to invade castles.

Many castles had what is known as a moat to protect them. A moat was a deep, broad ditch that was either dry or filled with water surrounding the castle. Many times, there was a draw bridge that people working in the castle would lower and close to allow people into the castle, and they would close it to keep unwanted visitors out. The moat made it hard for people to invade the castle. We are going to learn how to do the same thing in this chapter. It's so important that we monitor what we allow in and out of our world, both internally and externally. It's important to protect your mind, your mental real estate, and to protect your heart. Learning how to do this will significantly help you detach from some of the ways you may have done things when thinking with the victim mindset and will benefit you in rising higher as a victor.

Now that you are thinking like a victor, we need to get you out there, letting the world also appreciate you as much as I appreciate you and you appreciate you. It's time for you to allow God's light to exude through you, allowing nothing to get in your way. It's time to armor up!

Soldiers, knights, and police officers all wear protective armor to protect themselves from individuals shooting at them. They wear bulletproof vests and other forms of protective gear to protect them from having any foreign and unwanted objects penetrating their bodies. They want to stay alive once the mission or shift is completed. We must do the same, but with our minds. Remember, we are no longer giving our mental real estate or mental kingdom keys over anymore, but that does not fully prevent invaders from permeating our thoughts and derailing us. As victors, we need to take this one step further and protect our mental real estate by metaphorically keeping God's armor on. Some people believe you take it on and take it off! No! You always keep it on!

Your armor needs to stay on, so you continue growing in Christ, bulldozing adversity, and continuing to live as a victor. Life will bring trials and tribulations—as a human who is breathing and living on earth, *you will experience suffering*. It's a guarantee, congratulations— we won the jackpot. Just kidding. We got to have fun!

We know adversity is going to happen, which is why it's crucial to wear this armor all the time, allowing it to become one with your thinking. When you have the armor on, the trials, tribulations, adversity, or suffering you may face will no longer stop you! Can you say *victory!*

That's the goal, right, to not allow anything to knock you off your horse or life course!

There are six articles of armor we must put on each day! These six things will help you stand firm against people who may be trying to bring you down, adversity, and spiritual attacks. There are rulers of darkness out there waiting to destroy you and get you back down to a victim's way of thinking. You might ask why, and it's because of your conviction to follow Christ.

Sometimes people who feel inadequate develop a belief of inadequacy when they are around positive, confident, self-assured, and Jesus-loving people. Now, when you praise God and allow Him to be your source of joy, contentment, and hope, expect to rile up a few spirits of darkness. The reality is following Christ can put a target on your back for people, evil spirits, or both to attack you.

Sometimes when we are first transforming our way of living from a low place of being to a high place, weird things will happen. You might notice tribulations may become more of a norm in your life for a bit. You might even notice opportunities where strife, tensions, stress, or worry are working their way over you. That's okay. I say that because it's merely the evil spirits trying to stop you from following God. Keep *resisting* by submitting to God! You can do it. Now, yes, sometimes you might fail, but that's okay. Some seasons require you to walk it out with Christ! Keep allowing Jesus to work in your heart, and you will get there!

Don't buy into the story of your life isn't going to get better. Please don't buy into the falsity that you don't deserve it, or it's never going to happen. They are all lies.

I am living proof of this. Everything I am encouraging you to do, I am doing or have done, and let me tell you— I have so much more joy in my heart now!

As I was transforming years ago, I remember when I felt like I was starting to get the hang of things, weird things would happen. The devil is going to try to stop you, and he's going to go for your most sensitive spots. For instance, it seemed more people had a problem with me, life would *feel* harder, I lost friends as my faith grew stronger, and overall I began to feel more persecution. It's like I couldn't catch a break. But, I promise, like everything external, it will pass. Trust God. Keep your eyes on Him. Keep speaking love and God's Word over yourself.

I hope this brings you a comforting perspective too. When you are transforming, and it appears the external world is working against you—celebrate that. Why? You're on the right track. If people begin to persecute you because you are so joyful, in love with Christ, and are mindful of the words you speak and thoughts you engage with—rejoice. These are all great things. Misery loves company, and the spirits of darkness do not want you to be victorious. Spiritual warfare is very real. Remember, we do not battle against flesh and blood but with the unseen spirits. Those conflicts are the spirits attacking one another. Spirits will come over people. Spiritual warfare wounds us the deepest in our hearts and minds. Become mindful of what you allow in this world to captivate you because it is not all good. If you aren't sure if you should be doing something or not, call out to the Holy Spirit!

The ways spiritual battles will present themselves are through thoughts regarding what you know to be true. When you learn how to conquer your mind—where two of your greatest opponents are—you can learn how to do anything. Your greatest opponents all come from the kingdom of darkness. Life is quite spiritual! You can be strong, confident, joyful, and exuding love all the time, even in the worst scenarios, if you allow Jesus' peace and love to grow inside your heart.

Putting on God's Armor

Since the devil couldn't care less about your prosperity, success, or cultivating a thriving life, he is going to do everything he can to stop you!

What do you do?

First, remember the devil has already been defeated! However, the enemy has done an excellent job of being a sore loser and perverting things. Think about it—most people pray about their problems when God says to pray for your solutions and desires.

---

*For assuredly, I say to you, whoever says to this mountain, 'Be
removed and be cast into the sea,' and does not doubt in his
heart, but believes that those things he says will be done, he
will have whatever he says.*
Mark 11:23 (NKJV)

Secondly, we must put on the armor of God and use it! Merely wearing the armor of God is not enough to defeat the enemy.

To learn what God's armor consists of, read Ephesians 6:10-18:

> In conclusion, be strong in the Lord [draw your
> strength from Him and be empowered through
> your union with Him] and in the power of His
> [boundless] might. Put on the full armor of God
> [for His precepts are like the splendid armor of a
> heavily-armed soldier], so that you may be able
> to [successfully] stand up against all the schemes
> and the strategies and the deceits of the devil.
> For our struggle is not against flesh and blood
> [contending only with physical opponents], but
> against the rulers, against the powers, against the
> world forces of this [present] darkness, against
> the spiritual forces of wickedness in the heav-
> enly (supernatural) places. Therefore, put on the

complete armor of God, so that you will be able
to [successfully] resist and stand your ground in
the evil day [of danger], and having done everything [that the crisis demands], to stand firm [in
your place, fully prepared, immovable, victori-
ous]. So stand firm and hold your ground, having tightened the wide band of truth (personal
integrity, moral courage) around your waist and
having put on the breastplate of righteousness
(an upright heart), and having strapped on your
feet the Gospel of peace in preparation [to face the
enemy with firm-footed stability and the readiness produced by the good news]. Above all, lift up
the [protective] shield of faith with which you can
extinguish all the flaming arrows of the evil one.
And take the helmet of salvation, and the sword of
the Spirit, which is the Word of God.
With all prayer and petition pray [with specific re-
quests] at all times [on every occasion and in every
season] in the Spirit, and with this in view, stay
alert with all perseverance and petition [interced-
ing in prayer] for all God's people.

Ephesians 6:10-18 (AMP)

God really does have all the answers. Now, let me explain the application of His armor!

The Belt of Truth

What is the first thing Paul tells us to put on? The belt of truth. Think of the belt of truth as accurate or correct living, living God's way. Remember, the devil will fight you with lies. He will twist, manipulate, and pervert God's truth. Therefore, we must decipher or discern information concerning God's Word. The belt of truth prepares one to be ready for action. We are always to be prepared to fight the enemy off.

How can you prepare yourself in every circumstance? By making sure that you are a person of truth. You must know God's truth. That means knowing the good news about Jesus, understanding in your heart why you believe in Jesus, and living as a person of integrity as someone honest and trustworthy.

I am always amazed at how quickly people accept and agree with the words spoken over, at, or to them. You must be careful deciding with others before you have thought about it or gone to the Word of God. Instead of just foolishly agreeing with people on unfamiliar areas you are unsure about, say the following instead:

"I hear what the person is saying regarding this subject. I don't know if that is true or simply their truth. Since I seem curious about it, I am going to look into what they are saying before I go any further with participating with their thoughts."

It is crucial to apply God's truth to all the enemy's lies. I encourage you to start adopting a God filter, where you run everything you hear through God and His Word before buying into it.

Just as God needs a vessel (a body), so does the devil and his principalities of darkness. Sometimes, people forget that the devil and his minions will use people to try to get to you more times than not! It may feel as if we are fighting against flesh and blood, but we are not. More than likely, that person has opened themself up to be used by powers of darkness. They cannot have power unless someone allows them into their body. Remember, most of the world is lost and evil. People have unknowingly opened their bodies to the most disgusting and destructive thing—the devil and his principalities of darkness.

Let me give you an example of how people fail to use the belt of truth. Many people are afraid—the Spirit of Fear is dominant in most people. When they are confronted with whichever specific Spirit of Fear (fear of failure, man, rejection, etc.) they struggle with, many flee. But God's Word says the enemy is to flee from you (James 4:7; Deuteronomy 28:7)! You are to tell the enemy to go! How do you do that? By saying, *"In the name of Jesus, I bind the devil and all his principalities of darkness, and I command you to go! You have no authority in or over me! I cast out the Spirit of Fear in the name of Jesus, and I allow the peace and joy of the Lord into my heart!"*

You can investigate it by asking for the Holy Spirit's help, reading the Word, and prayer. The Godhead is here to help you.

Breastplate of Righteousness

The second piece of God's armor is the breastplate of righteousness! First, let's unpack the word righteousness concerning the Word of God. Righteousness means "right standing with God." Doing things God's way, not the world's way! The old English of righteousness is "right" and means wise, way, or manner. When you begin to trust and like yourself, you may find yourself operating more in your God-given gifts and talents. From there, your ability to discern wisdom will significantly grow, and I encourage you to practice that. The more you do something, the easier it becomes. The more you do it, the better you will get!

Now here is where things can get tricky. It would be best if you remember your worth. You must retain your worth concerning God and how God sees you, not how you see yourself. You must remember, in God's eyes, you are fantastic, excellent, and loved! You must remember that God will never leave you nor forsake you and that He is always with you regardless of whether you feel it.

Part of successfully wearing God's armor is remembering how much God loves you.

Here's the thing, God offers His righteousness to every believer in Jesus Christ (Titus 3:5; Philippians 3:9). If God offers His righteousness to every believer in Jesus Christ, then what does it mean to put on and successfully wear the breastplate of righteousness?

Well, first, it's choosing to believe and accept Jesus Christ as your Lord and Savior. It's understanding in your heart, not your mind. Knowing you cannot be righteous with God until you see Jesus as your Lord and Savior—as the Son of our Father in heaven. It's learning to stand firm against injustice and corruption. Isaiah is a beautiful chapter in the Bible that talks about doing things even if you sense fear. It's choosing to move forward even with the sensation of fear and trusting God to be your advocate and protector. Lastly, it's knowing that God promised His protection against evil forces for those who have faith in Jesus.

"But since we belong to the day, let us be sober,
putting on the breastplate of faith and love, and the
helmet of our hope of salvation"
(1 Thessalonians 5:8, ESV).

The application of wearing the breastplate of righteousness is more about walking in faith, your beliefs, and how much you apply God's word in your life. If you're a part-time believer, you're going to get part-time results.

The Shoes of Peace

Victors believe that when you allow God's peace to rule in your heart, you will become motivated to tell people about all the marvelous things God is and has done for you. Additionally, it becomes easier to renew your mind, stand, trust, and believe in God and His promises.

The Greek word rendered *"preparation"* or *"readiness"* in Ephesians 6:15 can also be translated as "prepared foundation"—in other words, a firm basis for a soldier's feet. Just as the hobnails allowed the soldiers to stand firm—preparing your feet with the Gospel of peace will also help you stand firm in spiritual battles! When your feet are wearing the peace of God, nothing can make you slip, tremble, or fall!

The Gospel is the good news that you can have peace with God. Remember, Jesus is the Prince of Peace!

Before you turned to Jesus, most likely, you wanted to live for yourself. I would bet that internal peace was quite absent in your life too. When you do not care about God's plan and how God encourages you to live, you become in conflict, believe it or not. You must remember that God loves you and made way for you to be reconciled with Him, and when you are reunited with Him, you can begin to live in peace.

How do you start to receive Jesus's peace? Perfect peace belongs to those whose *minds are fixed or stayed on the Lord.*

"You will keep him in perfect peace, Whose mind is stayed on You, Because he trusts in You" (Isaiah 6:23, NKJV).

It's the absence of conflict. Remember, the Lord wants believers to live in peace and unity with one another. We are called to be peacekeepers. It's absent of worry. This peace is the confidence that God has everything under control, and you can trust Him. Are you willing to cast all your concerns, cares, anxieties onto Him? Do you believe He truly cares for you?

The Shield of Faith

Before I specifically discuss how to apply the shield of faith into your life practically. I want first to discuss and break down the word "faith." Faith is a word from the mid-13th century, meaning "faithfulness to trust or promise; loyalty to a person, honesty, truthfulness." From the Anglo-French and Old French *feid, foi* means "faith, belief, trust, confidence, pledge." The Latin word *fides* means "trust, faith, confidence, reliance, credence, belief." Take all those breakdowns and assemble them together, and you are left with: *to place your trust and loyalty with confidence into a belief.* That is what we must work to grow our faith in God, His Word (Jesus), and the Holy Spirit.

When you have faith in God and maintain that loyalty or confidence, you begin to protect yourself from the fiery arrows of spiritual attacks. The real cool thing is when you bring God into this place of spiritual attacks, you can start to see the real battle—that it's not between flesh and blood, but it's between the unseen things of our world. When that person calls you names, hurts you, or puts you down, you will see that it is not that person but dark spirits within that person—ever talked with someone who was battling the Spirit of Fear? They can be mean!

You can see beyond the circumstance—the attack of what is occurring right now—and you start to see the ultimate victory is already yours. Now, as victors, this is awesome, right? Because we are *victors*, we have victory when we rest and trust in God.

The shield of faith will protect us from the arrows of the evil one—think spiritual attacks or spiritual warfare—and us from temptations. The way to successfully utilize the shield of faith when tempted is to trust that God will provide everything, including a way out.

Sometimes before the spiritual attacks or warfare, there is some thought or belief that the enemy tries to sell you on. It's essential to use this shield of faith to combat such lies. However, that's not enough. I hate to say it, but it's true. To be a successful soldier of Jesus, you must get in the Word of God not only to learn the promises that God has given you but also how Jesus thinks. To operate in Christ's mind, you need to know how Jesus and God think, and that's the power of reading the Bible and implementing it into your life.

The Helmet of Salvation

Life can get hard, stressful, and overwhelming when we take our eyes off God's Word and Jesus' ways. Some days it can feel like the world is screaming at you, *"You suck! You're doing everything wrong! You are never going to amount to anything. You don't do enough."*

All of this can create doubt, guilt, and confusion in a person, which is all fruit of the devil! The enemy is working on getting you to doubt God's ways, so you will abandon them and never reach God's best and promises in your life! He wants to steal all your life from you!

These messages in the world can get loud, and it is easy to buy into them. Please don't! Much of what we are to do as disciples are opposite from what the world encourages! If the world's opinion was right, wouldn't we have more prosperity, peace, and love flowing within the world? God's way is the *only* way to everlasting peace, prosperity, health, and eternal life. Therefore, we need something to protect us and separate us from our doubts, doubts of the enemy, or people's doubts.

Salvation is God's ultimate victory over the spirits of darkness! God redeemed His people by using Jesus' death on the cross and the resurrection. God's selfless choice to allow His Son to be brutally and inhumanely beaten broke the power of death. Now we have freedom from sin and eternal life in heaven. The helmet of salvation points directly to that—the victory to that defeat!

The helmet of salvation means Jesus saved you out of grace, not because you deserve it! As long as you live for Christ, you will face battle and persecution for your beliefs. Accept and be happy about this. Understand and be thankful for your eternal life. God forgives you and cleanses you from all the wickedness.

The Sword of the Spirit

The belt, breastplate, shoes, shield, and helmet were used to protect against the enemy; therefore, these were defensive pieces of protection. Yet, the sword was designed to defeat the enemy's plans and rescue lives. To translate this into the application of what it means today, we have to focus on what Paul meant by *"the word."*

When you see *"word of God,"* there are typically a few meanings meant by the word *"word."* Either the writer is saying Logos or Rhema, which both mean *"word"* in Greek. However, in Ephesians 6:17, Paul is saying Rhema, which signifies the spoken word. To use the sword of the spirit, you must *speak* the Word of God.

The preached Gospel, the power of God, is the weapon provided by the Spirit of God for meeting the lunges of the assailant and beating him back. Uttering the Word of God is how truth is revealed. Combat is not against fellow humans; this is a truth that is easy to forget when you only see through your carnal eyes. The battle is only against the enemy, who has many ways of appealing to lost souls.

When the devil tempted Jesus, he used Bible verses toward the enemy. He didn't sit down and think about what the devil was trying to sell Him. He used His authority and His weapon—the Word of God—to get the devil to leave Him.

The Missing Piece

If you flip to Ephesians 6:18, we learn the missing piece that will *always* protect you. Paul is telling you to pray! Stand in prayer because, without prayer, God's armor is inadequate. If you do not continually pray while wearing God's armor, you will not obtain victory. Don't we see Jesus remain in prayer with the Father?

There are times where I have not had victory while wearing God's armor because I forgot to pray. I forgot to focus on God's power. I was too busy worrying about the enemy. My eyes were not set on the things above.

God's armor becomes inadequate if you fail to pray. Paul is telling you that prayer is vital! Without constant prayer—without constantly meditating on the Word of God or talking to God—your armor won't work. Prayer does not need to be as complicated as we humans can make it. Simply acknowledging God and asking Him what He wants you to do or letting Him know what's going on in your heart are great ways to stay in constant communication with Him.

Prayer is supernatural. It is that supernatural power that is released through prayer that "activates" your armor. Paul encourages you to pray when you are experiencing attacks of the enemy. In Philippians, he tells us not to worry about anything but to pray and give thanks! God wants to know your requests. God wants to talk with and to you. God wants your gratitude, your love, your appreciation, and an invitation into every area of your life. Are you giving the Father praise, thanksgiving, and that invitation?

Those are the six mental armors you need to place on yourself every day until they become our way of life. You got this. You are a victor. I hope this was helpful. I hope as you begin to participate with this armor, in time, you notice a huge difference with what you allow into your heart and with how you view life.

Prayer: Father God, teach me how to wear Your armor effectively. Raise me up to be a strong soldier in Your army! Please give me the revelation that I am only fighting against evil spirits and nothing else. Father, help me be more spiritually mature, wise, and patient in all that I do. In times where I want to fight with a person, please remind me of the truth. If I take Your armor on and off, remind me that I never need to take it off. Father, help me to do Your will in everything and show me how I can glorify You in all that I do. In Jesus' name, amen!

CHAPTER 22

Guarding Your Heart

Part of living as a victor means guarding your heart, as the Bible tells us.

> *"Guard your heart above all else,*
> *for it determines the course of your life"*
> (Proverbs 4:23, NLT).

Your heart, meaning your feelings, intellect, will, and desires, significantly dictate how you live in every area. Jesus clarifies that evil people bring evil things out of the evil stored in their hearts, whereas good people bring good things out of the good stored up in their hearts. The fruit of a person will be dependent on what is inside the individual.

What you allow to take root inside of you is more important than anything you will ever say or do. Again, what you say and do reveals your true beliefs, attitudes, motivations, and desires. The truth is you will find the time to do what you love and enjoy. It's human behavior always to find the time to do the things you want. If you are not sure of what you enjoy doing, well, this is an optimal opportunity to begin mindfully paying attention to all the things you will put above God's will and hopes for you. Also, pay attention to the excuses you say as to why you can't do what God is asking you to do! What are you putting ahead of God?

Unfortunately, some things people love can be dangerous and destructive, leading them to death, not life. It is easy for people to fall in love with worldly desires as opposed to godly desires. Lust can feel quite convincing and convicting. If this is happening to you, keep asking the Lord to change your heart, helping you to kill that desire. It may take time, but He is always faithful.

One thing victors are highly protective over is their morning time with God. They know how crucial it is to start and end their day with God. They make time to read the Bible, pray, and meditate on scripture. While sometimes they may only be able to spend fifteen-twenty minutes with the Father, they prefer and set their calendars accordingly to spend as much time in the mornings as possible. Additionally, they desire to remain in communication with the Father all day long and end their day with the Father too!

Both Solomon and Jesus stress the importance of watching or guarding your heart above all else. Guarding your heart is simpler than you may imagine. You can guard your heart by concentrating on the desires that will keep you on the right path. These desires are the ones that come from God. To know these desires, you must spend time with the Father. You must be willing to surrender over to God all the desires and thoughts that are not of Him. You must also stop being curious about evil and become more mindful to what you expose yourself to with the help of the Holy Spirit. The Father will help you in this. It is God who can take any desires that are not of Him and remove them from you.

All humans are born as sinners. Our human nature prefers to please ourselves rather than God, which is why we must rely on Him. Start asking God to cleanse your heart and spirit. Victors understand that their flesh will try to get in the way of God's will for their life, which is why they constantly ask the Father for Him to pour His desires and thoughts into their hearts. When you allow God to cleanse you, He starts to renew your entire inner self. As you allow God to do this, it will become more natural for you to guard your heart because you will be able to discern what is from Him and what is not quickly.

Sometimes our flesh wants us to do things that God doesn't want us to do. Therefore, we must put boundaries and even implement discipline when our eyes lust over things. Part of walking on the righteous path is allowing God to guide you in all your choices. For God to guide you on all your choices, you must invite God into all your decisions. It is about asking Him what is best for you to do instead of making your own decisions. You are to be completely dependent on God and be grateful for this partnership. You must keep your eyes fixed on Him. It can be easy to get sidetracked, but it becomes more difficult when you keep your eyes on Jesus.

Paul tells us in Romans 12:1 that we are to give our bodies to God because of all He has done for us, encouraging us to be a living and holy sacrifice that is acceptable to Him as this is truly the way to worship our Father! One way you can exemplify this is through being obedient from the heart. Victors understand that following Christ means they may have to place down their desires, goals, and wishes to follow Him. It is giving God all your energy, efforts, and resources for His disposal, choosing to trust Him to guide you.

The reality is God wants to live in your heart if you allow Him to. He wants to live in the hearts of those who love Him. When you know God is in your heart, you begin wanting to protect your heart even more because of the precious cargo inside. He lives inside of you as the Holy Spirit. Think about how protective a pregnant mother is over her unborn child. She is cognizant to follow the doctor's requirements to carry a healthy baby. She will refrain from alcohol, smoking and even become more mindful of what she eats and her overall health. The same needs to happen when we allow God into our hearts. Start protecting your temple!

As you work to grow as a victor and your mindset changes, please expect to lose interest in certain friends, hobbies, and lifestyles you currently participate in. You are going to transform not just in your thinking but also in how you spend your time. It's pretty awesome. You might start realizing how important it is to take care of yourself physically, allowing exercise to become a routine of yours. Or maybe the Holy Spirit will help you recognize that friend you spend a lot of time with is very negative and toxic, encouraging you to spend less or no time at all with them. Sometimes stepping away from certain people is a temporary thing as the Lord works to help you become a more mature and focused Christian. He might encourage you to go back to that friend once you are a stronger believer. Whatever it is, He will tell you!

Others may notice you are no longer interested in listening or doing things you once thought were fun. This might sound daunting, but it's also a fabulous place to be. Why? Because you are living for God now, not for man! That's awesome. Rejoice!

Sometimes we have to remove family members from our lives or people we have known for decades due to how that individual chooses to live their life. Other times, God will encourage you to leave a family member so healing can take place. It's not always a bad reason, but one that will help you have life in the long run. Trust Him. Again, it might be a temporary disconnect or a permanent one, but whatever happens, know it will be organic. God is quite the gentleman.

When your friends' or family members' lives start to conflict with your values, beliefs, and mindsets, it's okay to leave them for the greater good.

A large crowd was following Jesus. He turned around and said to them, "If you want to be my disciple, you must, by comparison, hate everyone else—your father and mother, wife and children, brothers and sisters— yes, even your own life. Otherwise, you cannot be my disciple. And if you do not carry your own cross and follow me, you cannot be my disciple.
Luke 14:25-27 (NLT)

You may even notice it's not enjoyable to be around that person. Typically, these relationships balance out quite naturally, but if you must be firmer and more direct with a friend, please do so with love and encouragement. Whether or not that friend reciprocates the feelings is neither here nor there. The worst-case scenario is the friend will attack you and speak cruel things about your new way of living. If that happens, you just learned a lot! Be grateful! Pray for them and give it to God. Do not allow the cruel words to affect you—remember the armor you put on. Notice the negativity and victim thinking of their attitude. If that does happen, it's confirmation that separating yourself from that person is quite intelligent.

Remember, people will try to hurt you as you go through your life. But you are a victor—so you get to choose if those words have power or not over your life. As you guard your heart, it's even more important to speak life and not corrupt speech. Remember, God is living inside of you! Of course, you might slip. That's okay. By no means am I saying you have to live perfectly. I merely advocate that you become more aware of your tendencies and give the fleshly ways over to God to change. When you love something, you want to protect it. When you love God, you want to protect yourself, others, and your relationship with Him.

Somehow, someway swear words became "*cool.*" It's like what smoking was in the '60s and '70s. Smoking was cool, but later they found it was incredibly damaging to their health. Speaking inappropriate words and swearing is the same. I am guilty of this from time to time, but I am immensely better. It's not about arriving.

It's about setting out on the journey so you can arrive. Do not gossip about people either. Gossip and speaking foul language will penetrate your armor. By participating in perverse talk, you are putting holes into your armor. You are creating permanent bridges over your moat (*remember the space that protects your kingdom from invaders*) that invaders will take advantage of.

Keep claiming, receiving, and believing the truth and life over yourself. Be open to God in all ways. As you keep your eyes on what lies ahead, make sure you have marked a path for your feet to get there, and keep to that path. If you aren't sure where God wants you to go, spend some time in prayer clarifying what He's asking of you. Sometimes God will tell you the big picture, and sometimes He will only share enough information for you to advance one space forward. Whatever He shares with you, choose to respond obediently. As you do this, you will notice your single-mindedness will increase. Do not let anyone get you off God's path. Anyone trying to take you away from what God is telling you to do is not of His kingdom, which is why it's so important you trust yourself to trust God. There may be times where a believer tells you not to do what the Lord is telling you to do.

Here's the thing, God will speak to you about things that others have no idea about. Other believers might put it down due to their own biases. Only you know what God has told you. Now, if you are married, God will confirm it to both of you. Same for the parent-child relationship. The other thing is God will never go against His word. If you are not sure if what you are hearing is from God, start reading your Bible or start walking with an older, wise follower of Christ to help you discern the situation. The Bible encourages us to have elders to help us grow in our discipleship. But, as you keep living this way, you will begin to identify your strengths and what your purpose is.

In closing, pray and remain alert to the truth and your life's focus, which needs to be living for Jesus. That broad scope will become more narrow and clearer to what you specifically are to do in His kingdom. Stay single-minded.

Understand people, things, hobbies, and life will try to get you off track. Even people you confide in will try to take you off your path in ways that sometimes look as if they are helping you. This is why you have to guard your heart and trust God so you can discern when someone brings you a brilliant idea or a distraction. Always consult the Father. When God wants you to do something, you will have peace in your spirit. It's quite surreal, as your flesh might be freaking out or in a state of fear, but your spirit will be calm and full of peace and contentment.

Contemplate what is or might influence you before you expose yourself to things. For instance, I would allow the opinions of some Christians to take me away from God's will for my life. Deep in my heart, I knew what I was doing was from God, but some of these believers had deep biases that were not biblically correct. They would tell me becoming a therapist was evil or marrying my husband was wrong because they didn't like him. Thank God, God redeems all things. Since I cared more about confirmation from a human instead of taking steps of faith, I stalled a few things and made some problems for my life. However, I never stopped praying about what God wanted me to do. As I grew wiser, closer to God, and grew my biblical understanding, I learned that God did want me to do the things that a few Christians marked as "bad." You cannot let humans make the final say. Only God gets that. Some of the things God's asking you to do will not make sense to others because He's telling you things in your spirit that you can't always communicate effectively. It requires taking a leap of faith and trusting God to reroute you if you were, in fact, wrong. Now there are times where we do mistake the devil for God, which is why I encourage you to consult the Bible before you move too. The Bible and God will never contradict each other.

It's so essential you maintain your focus and concentration on the desires that will keep you on the right path. You know when you're on the right track or not, even if you don't want to admit it. Make sure everything you do and say is centered around love and doing life God's way. Put boundaries around your desires too. Don't go after everything you see. Don't agree with every good idea that comes to you. Sometimes it's not from God. The reality is to start paying attention to the motivation behind the action. What is driving you? Is it fear or love? When God asks you to move, it won't be due to fear but love. In all that, you do first seek the kingdom of God. God knows when you have a sincere heart or not.

Look straight ahead, keep your eyes fixed on your goals while staying agile and open to God redirecting you. Consult God on everything and quickly watch your world transform for the greater!

Prayer: Father God, help me to keep my eyes fixed on You. Please help me understand and desire to guard my heart. Help me to live life Your way and not my way. I want Your will to be done in every aspect of my life. Do whatever You need to do inside of me for that to happen. Please use me. Please grow me. Please make me one with You. In Jesus' name, amen.

CHAPTER 23

You Got This!

Congratulations on completing this book! You stuck with it, and there is something to be said for that! If you are feeling overwhelmed or wondering if you can do all this, please know you can. That overwhelm is not coming from God's kingdom but the enemy. Tell it to go in Jesus' name. The reason you can do this is because God wants you to live and see yourself as victorious. Now, your definition and His may differ, but He wants you to be blessed, prosperous, and full of life and love.

Here's the thing. You cannot do any of these changes without the help of Jesus. He will do so much of the work if you allow Him, but you must accept Jesus' yoke.

Then Jesus said, "Come to me, all of you who are weary and carry heavy burdens, and I will give you rest. Take my yoke upon you. Let me teach you, because I am humble and gentle at heart, and you will find rest for your souls. For my yoke is easy to bear, and the burden I give you is light."
Matthew 11:28:30 (NLT)

Jesus offers all rest who come to Him in childlike faith. Have you ever watched a child believe or have faith? It's incredible! Learn from them! The rest Jesus is offering you is the freedom of religious law and legalism. Jesus wants to give you joy, peace, healing, everlasting love, and eternal life with Him. Let Him be a part of every aspect of your life. Invite Him fully into your heart and life. Do not keep any part of you from Him!

The Victor Transformation is merely one way you can begin to create a strong foundation in Christ. The best choice you can make is living for Jesus. When you make that decision, your world will start to transform for the better naturally. However, you must put your faith to work too. James tells us that faith without works is dead. Jesus reminds us that we will know His disciples by their fruit. The thing is, sometimes life has a *walking-it-out with Jesus* season. Sometimes, it takes time to renew your mind in a certain area. That's okay. In these seasons, give yourself grace and keep asking God to change you.

The best encouragement I can give you is to ask the Father where you need to start and focus on that. Trying to do everything in this book at once will be overwhelming. Make small steps. Start slow. Maybe right now, the best thing you can start doing is remembering to keep your eyes on Jesus all day long. That small shift in perspective is huge in itself. It can be difficult to remember to focus on Jesus when you are out and about in the world. If you find yourself doing more worldly behavior than you want, then ask the Father to help you keep focused on Him. Do your best to have a Jesus filter, where you mentally ask yourself, *What would Jesus say about what I am doing right now?*

The bottom line is, Jesus cares more about your walk than your talk. He would rather you do the right thing than give lip service.

I pray this book has blessed you in teaching you how to build your house (yourself) on rock and not sand. Life storms are coming, but those who build their life on the foundation of Jesus Christ will not fail.

As a sister in Christ, I believe in you, and I am praying for you! You got this!

Prayer: Father God, Thank You for Your Son and for loving me so much that You let Jesus endure the pains and torture for me to have eternal life with You. I want to live for You. I want a strong foundation that is built only on You. I need Your help transforming my life. Please show me where I need to be focusing my time, attention, and faith. I invite you fully and completely into my heart and every area of my life. You have my permission to knock down every wall I have and to free me from my bondage. As I move through today, help me to glorify You in everything I do. Father, please help me keep my eyes and heart locked only on You. I ask You to remove everything that is not of You from me. Father, please send me the people, hobbies, and career that You want me to have. Please guide me in everything! Show me when I am living for the world and not for You. In Jesus' name, amen!

About Renew Ministries

Renew Ministries is an online ministry that teaches believers how to engage in mental health issues and emotional wellness from a biblical perspective and how God's Word is relevant to one's life today. We focus on renewing believers' minds to the Word of God and developing Warriors for Christ. We do this by sharing the Gospel, explaining the spiritual components of mental health, and teaching the application of the Word across the world. In short, we focus on healing mental health issues and emotional wellness from a biblical perspective, with the support of biblically accurate psychology and neuroscience principles.

We focus on transforming people by renewing their minds through teaching how God's Word relevantly applies to their life today, teaching people the spiritual components behind every mental health issue, and how to be victorious in God's armor. At Renew Ministries, we remind one another that we do not fight against flesh and blood but against principalities, powers, and rulers of darkness.

To learn more about Renew Ministries, please visit RenewMinistries.org. Please follow us @RenewMinistriesOnline on Instagram and Facebook. Check out our podcasts—*THE reNEWed YOU!* podcast, which you can find on all major podcast apps or on our website.

If you have any questions or concerns, email us at Info@RenewMinistries.org

About the Author

Elizabeth Louis Creecy works as a teacher of God's Word, professional mental health coach, and pastoral counselor. She is currently earning a MA in Clinical Mental Health Counseling, where she will then become a Licensed Professional Counselor (LPC). She is the headteacher at Renew Ministries, where she is passionate about teaching believers how to renew their minds to the Word of God and empowering believers to become Warriors for Christ!

As a lover of Jesus Christ, Elizabeth writes and teaches about the gospel, how the Bible applies to one's life today, and how to achieve optimal mental and emotional wellbeing by leveraging biblical principles and cultivating a deep relationship with Jesus Christ. She hosts THE reNEWed YOU! podcast, where she teaches people how to navigate psychological, emotional, and wellbeing matters through the lens of Jesus. Elizabeth believes the Bible has all of life's answers and that one must be cautious when leveraging psychology.

After earning an MS in Positive Psychology, Elizabeth began to see the holes of psychology. Some psychology is demonic, which has fueled her to teach others a more excellent way to freedom. Today, she advocates that the only way to heal and experience freedom is by doing life the way Jesus did.

Elizabeth lives and works out of her home in Richmond, Virginia, where you will find her dog, Moo-Moo, right next to her. She and her husband, Austin, enjoys the outdoors and spreading the gospel wherever they go.

Bibliography

Aandoiu, A. (2018, March 23). Why self-love is important and how to cultivate it. *Medical News Today.* Retrieved from https://www.medicalnewstoday.com/articles/321309.php

Branden, N. (1992). *The Power of Self-Esteem.* Deerfield Beach: Health Communications.

Brown, B. (2012). *Daring Greatly.* New York, NY: Avery.

Burton, N. (2015). Self-confidence versus self-esteem. Retrieved from https://www.psychologytoday.com/us/blog/hide-and-seek/201510/self-confidence-versus-self-esteem

Clinton, T. E., & Sibcy, G. (2006). *Why You Do the Things You Do: The Secret to Healthy Relationships.* Nashville, TN: Thomas Nelson.

Clinton, T., & Hawkins, R. (2009). *The Quick-Reference Guide to Biblical Counseling.* Grand Rapids, MI: Baker Books.

Definition of self-esteem. (2018). Retrieved from https://www.merriam-webster.com/dictionary/self-esteem

Definition of Victim mentality. (2019). Retrieved from https://www.merriam-webster.com/dictionary/victim%20mentality

Definition of Victim. (2019). Retrieved from https://www.merriam-webster.com/dictionary/victim

Farstad, A. (Ed.). (2016). *Believer's Bible Commentary* (2 ed.). Nashville, TN: Thomas Nelson.

Holy Bible - King James

Holy Bible - *Life Application Study Bible*, New Living Translation

Hopper, A. (2018). *Dynamic Neural Retraining System: Retrain Your Brain, Transform Your Health, Reclaim Your Life*. [DVD]. Victoria, British Columbia, Canada: Author

Kim, S., & Gal, D. (2014, August 1). From compensatory consumption to adaptive consumption: The role of self-acceptance in resolving self-deficits. Journal of Consumer Research, 526-542. Retrieved from http://eds.a.ebscohost.com/eds/pdfviewer/pdfviewer?vid=4&sid=92ecc278-e901-4a76-9e5a-a0f3aa94246e%40sdc-v-sessmgr03

Kollar, C. A. (2011). *Solution-Focused Pastoral Counseling: an Effective Short-Term Approach for Getting Back On Track*. Grand Rapids, MI: Zondervan.

Leaf, C. (2013). *Switch on Your Brain*. Grand Rapids, MI: Baker Books.

Leaf, C. (2017). *The Perfect You: A Blueprint for Identity*. Grand Rapids, MI: Baker Books.

Mead, E. (2019). What is positive self-talk? Retrieved from https://positivepsychology.com/positive-self-talk/

Medlock, G. (2012). The Evolving Ethic of Authenticity: from Humanistic to Positive Psychology. *The Humanistic Psychologist*, 38-56. http://dx.doi.org/10.108 0/088723267.2012.643.687

Neff, K. (n.d.). Self-compassion-guided meditations and exercises. Retrieved from https://self-compassion.org/category/exercises/

Newberg, A., & Waldman, M. R. (2009). *How God Changes Your Brain*. New York: Ballantine Books.

Newberg, A., & Waldman, M. R. (2013). *Words Can Change Your Brain*. New York, NY: Avery.

Orloff, J. (2012). Strategies to Deal With a Victim Mentality. Retrieved from https://www.psychology-today.com/us/blog/emotional-freedom/201210/strategies-deal-victim-mentality

Osborne, R. E. (2013). Self-esteem. *Salem Press Encyclopedia of Health*, 4. Retrieved from http://eds.a.ebscohost.com/eds/detail/detail?vid=2&sid=9802399c-e101-4801-bd51-5696e1be7c15%40sessionmgr4007&bdata

=JnNpdGU9ZWRzLWxpdmUmc2NvcGU9c2l0ZQ%3
d%3d#AN=93872219&db=ers

Peale, N. V. (1961). *The Tough-Minded Optimist.* Engle-
wood Cliffs, NJ: Prentice-Hall.

Peterson, C. (2006). *A Primer in Positive Psychology.* New
York, NY: Oxford University Press.

Peterson, C. (2006). *A Primer in Positive Psychology.* Oxford: Oxford University Press.

Rodriguez, M., & Ebbeck, V. (2015). Implementing
self-compassion strategies with female college gym-
nasts. *Journal of Sport Psychology,* 44-53. http://dx.doi.
org/ 10.1080/21520704.2014.991052

Self-acceptance exercise. (n.d.). Retrieved from https://
www.smartrecovery.org/smart-recovery-toolbox/
self-acceptance-exercise/?highlight=self-acceptance

Smart Recovery. (n.d.). Unconditional self-acceptance.
Retrieved   from   https://www.smartrecovery.org/
smart-articles/unconditional-self-acceptance/

Smeets, E., Neff, K., Alberts, H., & Peters, M. (2014,
September 1). Meeting suffering with kindness: Ef-
fects of a brief self-compassion intervention for
female college students. *Journal of Clinical Psychology,* 794-807. Retrieved from http://eds.b.ebscohost.
com/eds/pdfviewer/pdfviewer?vid=6&sid=6db11ffa-
8c3a-4179-9e8b-eb3f3096c478%40pdc-v-sessmgr01

Unconditional self-acceptance (USA). (n.d.). Retrieved
from   https://www.smartrecovery.org/smart-arti-

cles/unconditional-self-acceptance/?highlight=self-acceptance

Ungvarsky, J. (2019). Shame (social emotion). In Shame (). Retrieved from http://eds.b.ebscohost.com/eds/detail/detail?vid=2&sid=cf1cee15-9538-40b1-a34d-0b99ccc1f11e%40pdc-v-sessmgr04&bdata=JnNpdGU 9ZWRzLWxpdmUmc2NvcGU9c2l0ZQ%3d%3d#AN= 121772915&db=ers

Watzpatzkowski, W. (2016). The victim mentality - What it is and why you use it. Retrieved from https://www. harleytherapy.co.uk/counselling/victim-mentality. htm

Zukauskas, R. (2019). Self-love. In Salem press encyclopedia. Retrieved from http://eds.b.ebscohost.com/eds/detail/detail?vid=1&sid=58512bf9-f090-499b-bbcf-c1b0821bdc6c%40pdc-vsessmgr04&bdata=JnN pdGU9ZWRzLWxpdmUmc2NvcGU9c2l0ZQ%3d%3d #AN=133861201&db=ers